Of Poetry
A Compilation of Poetry and Quotes

Written By Albert E. Vicent
Compiled By Jonathan Vicent

Order this book online at www.trafford.com
or email orders@trafford.com

Most Trafford titles are also available at major online book retailers.

Printed in the United States of America.

ISBN: 978-1-4269-5428-3 (sc)

Trafford rev. 03/07/2011

 www.trafford.com

North America & international
toll-free: 1 888 232 4444 (USA & Canada)
phone: 250 383 6864 ♦ fax: 812 355 4082

Forward

Take a few minutes from the busy times
to let your mind wander and take you
away - like magic thru poetry and
permit you to return fulfilled.
Have lovely days always.

Selections

Children's

Children's Index

Balloons

Balloons are small
Balloons are large
And balloons go screech
When you rub them hard.
And balloons fly close
And far away
If you don't - tie them
To a string - to stay.
But I like balloons
All colors of balloons
Because they are to me
So real to feel and see.
And they stay on a string, with me
To bring,
Most any old place -
That I want to be.

Dinosaurs

The dinosaurs were here before

But are not around here anymore.

The walked and ran

They swung their tails

They gnashed their big teeth

And played too.

And maybe… they could have danced…

If someone, asked them to.

Funny

Crows are funny birds to see

They play together playfully

And when they walk

Their heads go -

Bobbity up, bobbity down

Bobbity, bobbity, bobbity,

Bobbity up and down.

Fun

Old tires are fun

They are round

And they can roll

Some are small

Some are big.

You can hang them

From a tree - to make a swing

That's a fun, fun - "really" fun place to be.

Or you can lay them flat

Right on their side

To make a fort

And play inside.

Old tires are neat

And funny too -

Because, nobody wants them

They are always, there -

To play with you.

In The Sky

Airplane, airplane

In the sky

I see you, hear you

Going by.

And I sometimes wish -

That you would stop

To take me with you.

So I could see

What you see,

Way up high -

Where birds fly… in the sky.

Everywhere

Sand in my pockets

Sand in my shoes

Sand in my hair

About everywhere I choose.

Sure feels like sands everywhere.

Think I feel sand in my eye,

Oh me - oh my.

Real Nice

Blue sky - blue sky

I see blue sky,

Also sunshine high

Way up in the sky.

And clouds down low

Where treetops grow.

But with blue sky, sunshine

Some clouds too,

Maybe a real nice day

Just said - "hello" to you.

Sunshine

Sunshine lights cloudy places,

Makes lots of happy faces,

But,

When it's cloudy and gray,

Happiness goes away

Till,

The sunshine comes.

Tie

Would you help me
My shoe strings all mixed up
And won't come out right.
I twisted and pulled, and looped it
Like mom said to do
Would you help me please
I can't tie my shoe.

Your Shoes

Sand in your shoes
Feels all -
Scrunchy and bumpy
And lumpy too.
And it really is fun
To have sand
In your shoes
When you run.
But pour it out -
When you're through.

A Spider

Whenever a spider
I see
I never really know.
Whether he's coming
Or going
It's strange to me.
Because…
He has
So many legs to see
You see.
I don't know
Which way
They may go.

The Wind

The wind is blowing
Hard today.
It's blowing
All the clouds away.
Now I can see
They sky so blue.
And all the hills
And valleys
Too.

Cookies

If the world was made

Of cookies

All crumbly nice and sweet

And the mountains

Made of ice cream all melt-tly and,

Just right to eat

And the trees had leaves

Of popcorn

All warm in bags to hold

What a wonderful place

That would be -

Just to stroll thru

And see.

Because, cookies are special

There's no two the same

Like almonds - or toffee

Or sweet sugar canes

Oh the cookie world

That few can see…

What a wonderfully

Beautiful place…

That must be.

The Octopus And Frog

The octopus,

Has many legs.

A frog,

Has only two for jumping.

But,

A frog can croak,

And jump,

In the grass.

This,

An octopus,

Can

Never... do.

Night

Night prevails,

When day is done,

Paints things,

Its own way,

And,

Leaves,

With the sun.

My Shadow

This I know,
My shadow goes where I go,
Follows with me,
And…
Sees what I see
We walk,
We're together,
Like friends, should always be,
Because,
We trust each other,
My shadow,
And,
I.

The Star Dipper

I seen the star dipper last night
In the heavens so bright,
3 stars make the handle,
4 stars make the dipper,
Of the many stars,
God made in the sky.
He only made one large
Star dipper,
I wonder why.

Love

Love arrives,

Suddenly,

Burns furiously,

Leaves,

Slowly.

The Quiet

Listen to the quiet,

The wise, silent quiet,

That was here,

When dinosaurs lived,

When cave man lived,

When pharaohs reigned,

When Christ lived,

Seen time,

Begin, end, linger, suspend,

Listen,

To the eerie, pulse,

Of,

The quiet.

Days

Rainy days give fog and haze,
Grass and ducks like rainy days,
Drifting clouds with hazy sun,
Make lazy days,
But,
Give more fun,
I like the lazy days.

Try

Soap and water
To make bubbles
On a nice windy day.
And watch as they blow
Way up high -
Then sail quiet
Far, far away.
Is something that is nice
And a really fun thing to do.
Try it… maybe you will like it too.

Little Clouds

Little clouds
Little clouds
Way up high.
Drifting , drifting
In a blue sky.
You look like sheep
Way way up high.
Little clouds, little clouds
In a blue sky.

Worms

Worms are real squirmy
And live in the ground.
They make little holes
When they crawl around.
Then when it's rainy
With rain coming down
The rain fills up their holes
And things grow
All around.

Star Dipper

Oh

Star dipper

Up so high

Twinkling in the deep blue sky.

How I wish

I really knew.

Just why you

Are really

You.

Very Far

Little star

Little star

Up so high

And very far.

If you see me

Where you are.

Can we be friends?

From -

Oh

So far.

Sunshine Sunshine

Sunshine sunshine
High in the sky
Shine everyday
For my friends and I.

Sunshine sunshine
Move in the sky
So we can watch you
As you go by.

Sunshine sunshine
Pretty and bright
Where do you go
When it's dark at night?

Jump

Jump up high
Reach for the sky
Pull down a handful of sunshine…
Just for you and I.

To Be

A house to be
As 1, 2, 3.
Must flow with love
From you to me.

Jump A Rope

Jump a rope
Skip a rope
Jump real high.

Jump a rope
Skip a rope
You and I.

Jump a rope
Skip a rope
Tell your friends.

Jump a rope
Skip a rope
Lets be friends.

When It Rains

Just where does the butterfly go
When it rains?
Does it hide in a log
Or other small things?
I wish that I knew
For then I could see
Where the butterfly goes
When it rains on me.

Stones

Stones are in the ocean
Stones are here on land
Stones worn by weather
Make sand
Upon the land.

My Swing #1

My swing, my swing
I love my swing
It takes me high in the sky.
And lets me be
Just me
Any time
To fly in the sky
For free.
My swing, my swing,
Oh I love my swing,
And my swing
My swing
Loves me.

My Swing #2

Sailing away on my swing I go
Way up high in the sky.
Where I can see
Far away things and close to me.
On my swing
That I ride in the sky.

Any Town

Suns up
Suns down
Sleepy time
In any town.

Whenever A Spider

Whenever a spider
I see
You see
It's very confusing for me
To see.
Because…
A spider
Has so many legs to watch.
I never know whether he's going or coming
Or going to come
Right over
And sit with me.

The Leaves

A little green
A little brown
On the leaves I see.
Autumn is coming
And soon the leaves
Will fall to the ground
With me.

Ripples And Pebbles

Tiny ripples in the ocean.
Tiny pebbles on the land.
Create waves upon the ocean.
Comes from boulders
On the land.

Little Bird

Little bird
Little bird
I see you walking
All around.
Little bird
Little bird
Do you know
That I'm around?

The Butterfly

Oh the butterfly is a beautiful thing
With brightly colored
Slow moving wings.
That quietly moves the air
As it flies
Taking the butterfly
Thru the skies.
Whether it's high
Or
Whether it's low
Anywhere that it wants to go.

We Like You

We like you Mr. Moon
We like you very much.
And if you weren't
So very high.
We'd come and touch you -
In the sky.

Wiggle Dee

Wiggle dee, wiggle dee woggle dō
Are some very nice words to say
You twist your mouth
You twist your tongue
You twist your nose
All round and round.
And when you're
Just about all done,
The words come out
In a wiggle dee way.
Wiggle dee, wiggle deee, woggle dō
Some very nice words to say.

Eels

Slimmery, slithery, slippery eels
Swimming in waters nearby.
Slithering, slithering, slithering long
Under the open sky.
Slithering, slippering
Slippering, slippering
Slithery, slithery, slithery eels.

From La-Room-Pas

There once was a man from La-Room-Pas
Who ate
Wearing blue pet-a-lum-pas
One morning
Said he
I wonder
Dear me.
In La-Room-Pas are others
Dressed eating
Like me.

An Angleworm

An anglee, anglee, angleworm

Went angling by one day.

And said

My friend won't you join me

As I angle on my way.

All you have to do

Is clap your hands

Shuffle

And sway, sway, sway.

Saying

Angleworm, angleworm, be on your way.

I say my friend

Won't you join me today?

While I go

Angling, angling, angling

On my angleworm way.

Crippity

Crippity, crippity, crippity cree
Oh me, oh my, oh my, oh me.
I think I see the things I see
From what I see
Oh dearie me,
I really don't know what to see.
Crippity, crippity, crippity cree
Oh me, oh my, oh my, oh me.

Hop Along

Hoppity hoppity
On the ground.
Little frogs
They hop along
To a nice cool
Water spot
Where they croak
And sing…
A lot.

Water

Cold water
Hot water
Warm water too
I like water
Don't you too?

Over A Hill

I seen a little cloud
Peeking over a hill
In the blue
Of the sky
Far away.
And it stayed
And it stayed
And it watched
As I played,
Then it floated
Up into the sky.
Where it drifted away
As the clouds
Do each day.
From the hills
To the blue
Of the sky.

What Fun

Up the ladder
Down the slide
Oh what fun
And a slippery ride.

Teeter Totter

Teeter totter
Up and down
Down and up again
You see me
And I see you
And then we start again.

The Merry Go Round

Run real fast
Then jump right on
And go for a ride
On the merry-go-round
Round and round
Round and round
go for a ride
On the merry-go-round.

Feathers #1

Feathers lying on the ground
Tell us that a bird's around.
And…
That a bird
Said something to us.
As it passed by here
Today.

Plink

Plink the water
Plink the sink
Dripping water's
In the sink.

Floppity

Merrily merrily
In the sky
A helicopter's passing by.
Floppity floppity
Choppity hi.
I hear it say…
As it goes by.

Floppity Floppity

Merrily merrily
In the sky
A helicopter's passing by
Floppity floppity
Chop chop hi.
It says to me…
As it goes by.

A Helicopter

Floppity floppity
Choppity hi
Way way high
Up in the sky
A helicopter's, passing by.

See The Moon

All the stars
Up in the sky
Can see the moon
And so can I.

I See

I see the stars
I see the sky
I see the moon so bright.
The stars they twinkle
And with the moon -
Light up the sky, at night.

Watch The Sky

I like to watch the stars at night
They are so bright to me
And in the sky
Way up so high
They see
The things
I see.

Many Stars

The many stars, I see tonight
All twinkling down on me
Makes me feel
Real good inside
And big
And small
And me.

Spiders

Spiders, spiders
They are small
But some
Have long legs
And are tall.
And if…
A spider
Could only sing.
Why golly gee…
With all those legs
And things.
A spider
Could maybe dance
And everything.

The Birds

Oh see the birds
As they walk around
Their heads go bob-bit-ty
Up and down.
Then this way that way
That way this.
Looking watching
As they go
And eating only things
They know.

 ## Me And You

Play with me
I with you
Think with me
I with you
We'll be friends
All year thru
Me and you.

Rollerskate

Put one foot up
And one foot down
And roller skate
All over town.

This Way

With one foot this way
One foot that
You can roller skate
If you do.
Like that.

In The Air

Rollerskate here
Rollerskate there
With both feet down
Or one in the air.

The Same

The dark waits till light leaves.

Then paints everything.

Even little nooks

And crannies.

Look

The very same.

Wiggle-dee Wog-gull-dō

Wiggle-dee - wog-gull-dee - wig-gull-dō

Look up and touch your toes.

Wiggle-dee - wog-gull-dee - wig-gull-dō

Touch your hair and nose.

Wiggle-dee - wog-gull-dee - wig-gull-dō

Reach out and touch a friend.

Wiggle-dee - wog-gull-dee - wig-gull-dō

Lets start all over again.

Up And Down

Sit down
Up you go,
Up and down.
Ride the teeter totter
go up and down.
Look up in the sky
Then you see the ground.
Ride the teeter totter
Go up and down.

Is

The grass is green
The sky is blue
The stars are high
The moon is too.
The sun is hot
Ice is cold.
And...
A tree I see
Is awful
Old.

So Dark

The windows are so dark tonight
They shine with dark
In the light.

Moon

Moon moon
Pretty and bright
Where do you go
When it's
Day light

Play With Me

Please just come
And play with me
Then you can see
The things
I see.

Little Worm

Little worm
Little worm
I see you
On the ground
And a bird
Is watching you
As you move around.

Little Bird

Tell me little bird
In your way.
What the flowers
Have to say.
Did the honey bee
Fly this way?
Will a rainbow
Come today?
If you tell me
Little bird.
I'll remember\
Every…
Word.

Let Me Help

W-hoo w-hoo

Let me help you fly your kite

Said the wind.

Let me help you fly your kite

Re-al

High.

You can't see me

I'm the wind.

But I go real high

Let me help you

Fly your kite…

In the sky.

Went By

On the Earth

We went by

And passed right under

The moon in the sky.

Trees And Grass

Green trees
Green grass
You grow so big
So very fast.

Christmas

Christmas Christmas
People say
Is a very, very…
Special day.

Holidays #1

Thanksgiving
Christmas
New Years too
Please tell me
Just what to do?

Holidays #2

Thanksgiving

Christmas

New Years too

Holidays come and when they do

Tell me

In my way how you feel -

Are you happy too?

The Zebra

Oh, the zebra's an animal too

Looks like a horse

And knows it too

Stripes all over

This way and that

And horses are happy - zebras look like that

Hee haw - hee haw - hee haw

But zebras don't care what horse's say

Cause horses work while the zebras play

Hee haw - hee haw - hee haw.

A Bell #1

The gentle tinkling of a bell
The far off ringing of a bell
Is music for our ears
To tell.

A Bell #2

The gentle tinkling of a bell
The far off ringing of a bell
Is something for our eyes to feel
And music
For our
Ears…
To tell.

Soaring By

Little airplane
In the sky
Up so very very high
Thru my window
To the sky
I can hear you
Soaring
By.

In Wiggle Dee - Woggle Dee - Wiggle Dō

In wiggle dee - woggle dee - wiggle dō
It neither rains nor snows.
And wiggle dee, woggle dee, wiggle dō
Is where you want to go.
Because wiggle dee, woggle dee, wiggle dō
Is very far away
And…
In…
Wiggle dee, woggle dee, wiggle dō
Everyone can play - all day.

Children Small

Grown up people
Are so tall
When I look up to see.
They look like giants
In the clouds
To children small
Like me.

Feathers #2

Feathers kind of tell us
In a quiet kind of way.
What birds
Can't really tell us
Because birds
Don't talk our way.
That a bird
Said something to us
As he flew be here
Today.
And the feathers kind of tell us.
In a quiet
Kind of way.

Wiggle - Tee - Squeak

Wiggle - tee - squeak

And up we go

Wiggle - tee - squeak

And down.

The teeter totters

So much fun

As we go up and down.

We see the sun

We see the ground

We see the people

And all around.

Wiggle - tee - squeak

And up we go.

Wiggle - tee - squeak

And down.

One Little Fly

One little

It-see

Bit-see

Tiny little fly

Flying very quiet

In the great big sky.

Just where did he go

I really don't know

But he flew by here

A long time

Ago.

Day To Day

Foot steps thought covered
Are seen...
Footsteps thought seen
Are covered...
To many– day to day
Along the way.
Especially, children

Go

Slow snail

Go snail

Slow snail go

Where just where

Just where

Will you go snail

Slow snail where?

I know you don't care

You take your house

With you

Most anywhere you go

Snail is ok with you.

So, slow snail

Make a trail

A Butterfly

There goes a butterfly
In the sky
Oh so quiet, very very quiet
Flying by
Right over there
Look, look—listen, listen
Can you see it ?
Can you hear the butterfly
In the sky
Flying by.

Fun Selections

Fun Selection Index

Listening

Waiting for the dawn to come

When night still has its way

Listening to the oceans roar

Tho its still…

Not far away

Watching light pierce thru the dark

Light so near…

Yet far away

Listening, waiting

Camping, loving

Nature's…

Holiday,

At Sunset Beach.

To Survive

A cultural tapestry

That permits all

To survive

To come alive

To harm none

Would be beautiful

Cause we harm

And permit survival

Unheard of

In love

As the birds

That travel the world

A natural tapestry

Of love from above.

What We Find

What humans believe in
Would boggle the mind
The creative juices
Make us feel good
With what we believe in
That we find.
As long as it does no harm
To others
Its beautiful too.
And gives comfort
In what we do.
Maybe other animals too
Do what we do.
If communication would
Permit us to, explore
Gosh, what humans believe in -
Would boggle the mind
With what we believe in
That we find.

The Same

Tho the frost killed the trees
And new plants too
Strange…
They all seemed the same
When their life was thru.

The Mountain Stream

The mountain stream,
Runs fresh and clean
As it ambles,
Thru the mountains
Far and wide.
Tho,
It runs o'er rocks,
And flows through dirt.
Its,
Preserved by God,
And the true,
Mountain stream
Remains,
Fresh,
Clear
And clean.

Work

We work,

From birth,

We work,

Till death,

And

In between,

We take a breath.

To check,

Just when,

We really did begin

This,

Work

Work

Work

Work

Work

Work.

Age Going By

I,

Seen age going by

Moving fast going by

Grandma,

Went by,

On roller skates.

Straining cheeks,

Frightened eyes,

Heaving chest,

And,

Rolling thighs.

I, seen age, going by,

Moving fast,

Slipping past.

As,

Grandma,

Went

Zipping by,

On,

Roller

Skates.

To Like To Enjoy

To like a job
Is ok.
To enjoy a job
Is sublime
To like,
And enjoy
Your work
Is
Sheer ecstasy.

Auto Body Repair

Worked on my friends
Old auto today.
The car had been smashed
Many different ways.
If,
It could speak,
It perhaps would say.
Please stop,
Remold me.
I,
Just don't,
Feel right,
This way.

Rain

The rain waits
In fleecy clouds,
Falls to earth
In silken shrouds.
Wets the earth
And you and me.
Then,
Goes back to,
The clouds.
Where,
Its high,
And free.

Time

Why,

I never,

Seen the likes,

As such.

When,

I don't need time,

Why there's just too much.

When,

I need some time,

It goes right by.

Never,

Waits for folks,

Like I.

Why,

I, never seen,

The likes as such.

Daytime Moon

I've never,

Seen the sun,

In,

A night time sky.

But,

I seen the moon,

In the sky today,

A night time, moon

In the sky today.

It'll probably,

Be real, real dark tonight.

Because the moon,

Stayed up,

All day,

Today,

Thinking,

Noon today,

Was,

The middle.

Of the night.

A Poem

I guess that I will

Never see,

A poem that's written

Just like me.

Because,

In my face,

I do express

The lines

That time and care,

Have pressed.

But,

A poem does not,

Have a body like me.

It only,

Has words,

That,

People see.

So,

A poem,

Can never,

Be written,

continues.....

Just exactly,

Quite,

Like me.

Anger

Anger comes,

Dims ones view,

Soon,

Everything changes,

To a slanted,

Angered,

View.

The Wind

The wind blew the clouds

Across the sky,

Blew the birds as they flew by.

Shook the leaves,

On the wise old trees

Made the ocean waves run high.

Then,

Rested from its play,

And,

Went with the sun,

For,

A holiday.

Problems

Problems are like snow

They come and go.

If you frown

They stay around.

But,

If you are happy

In,

Any way,

Problems leave.

They,

Just won't stay.

Driven Happiness

A problem a day

Drives,

Happiness away.

Far,

Very, very,

Far

Away.

Trouble

Trouble,

Comes to good folks.

Trouble,

Comes to bad,

Trouble,

Trouble,

Trouble,

Worst,

Friend,

Man ever had.

A Star Fell

I,

Seen a star fall,

From the heavens one night.

Lighting the dark sky,

In its,

Quiet,

Flight.

Opportunity

Opportunity,
Doesn't last long
I,
Hesitated,
And now its gone.

"Ideas"

Come,
When they please
On,
A fleeting breeze
Catch them fast,
Because,
They don't last.

Choice

What, you have chosen.
The, things you do,
Follow,
With you.
Your,
Whole life,
Thru.

Sand

Sand on the beach,

Sand in my hair.

Sand in my pockets,

Sand everywhere.

Sand,

Sand,

Sand.

Water

Water here,

Water there,

I wonder if,

Water is,

On a far off star.

If,

Water ever covers the earth.

We,

Might be better off,

Living,

On a star.

From Birth

Majestic the birds
That fly in the air
Soaring so quiet on high.
They do see I think
The world so fair
All alone
In the wonder - of the sky.
Theirs - to be in the sky
Soaring quiet on high
Or to be on Earth
Is a choice from birth.
Majestic…
The birds
The Earth
And - the sky.

A Flower

Like a fragrance
Of a flower -
Love goes out
To others.
And leaves no doubt
As the fragrance
Of a flower.
Love has gone out
Touching -
Silent, fragrant, lovely
Soft,,,
Like a butterfly,
Flies.

Eternal

The way the clouds

Drift so noiselessly

The way the sunlight warms

New fallen morning dew

The way blossoms form

With new leaves

On spring trees

New fruit in summer

Bountiful harvest

In autumn.

Also the winters of memories

And happiness - are beautiful

Leaving a lovely

Chosen love

To remember - as eternal

Forever.

Blue

I seen the moon

In the sky today

I seen the sun

In the sky today

And the sun together

With the moon

In a deep blue sky

Maybe says hello

To the moon

As they pass

Way up high

I wonder, I wonder, I wonder

Don't you

If the moon, and the sun

Talk...if they pass

When the sky - is blue.

Show Me

Teach and show me the way

I'll follow,

I won't stray,

I may fall

But,

That's ok

Only,

Teach,

And,

Show me the way.

Humming Bird

Fluttering wings,

Motionless,

In the air,

The humming bird

Moves,

With care.

Moonlight

The soft moonlight
On the gentle ocean.
Glows so softly,
On,
The rippling water,
In,
The night.

The Path

The winding path, spirals,
Up the mountainside,
To the top.
Passing,
Trees,
Stones,
Grass,
Everything.
But, doesn't stop,
Till, it goes to the top.

To Do Things

Feel, hear, feel, smell
If we see,
Things might really be
If we hear,
Things might be near,
If we feel,
Things might be real
If we smell,
We can't really tell
But,
If we,
See, hear, feel, and smell,
Well,
Who knows.

To Finish

To start is one part,
To continue another,
To quit partway thru,
Is, quite easy to do.
But,
To continue from start
Going from,
One end to the other,
And finish it all.
Is the real thing to do,
See,
The whole,
Program,
Thru.

Twilight

The twilight slips in,

On

Silken pods

Paints the world

Fit

For gods,

Then leaves,

Again.

Desire

I want to see

I think,

The things that

Cannot be,

For,

If I see the things

That cannot be,

Then,

I can better understand all,

The things I see.

Others

Others,
Live, love, die…
The same as I…
But,
To love,
Is to die…
Why,
Why.

To Know

I don't think
There's much to see
And maybe
There's not much
To know.
That folks somewhere
And folks somehow.
Just
Wonder why
That its
Not so.

Echoes #1

Echoes,

Talk the same as I,

They say,

The same things,

"Why," as time goes by,

They,

May think,

The same as I.

Echoes #2

Echo,

You sound so clear…

Like you are near…

Maybe,

You're small

Or, - sometime

Not at all,

Or… are you me?

To Know

I don't think
There's much to see
And maybe
There's not much
To know.
That folks somewhere.
And folks somehow.
Just
Wonder why
That its
Not so.

To Relax

Eating and sleeping
This
We must
Do.
But…
To relax
And enjoy life…
Not many…
Folks
Do.

Me Too

Lets pretend

Tho…

It may be true

If you think

The way I do.

That…

The only things

We really

Want to see.

Are things

That are really…

Nice to see.

And folks

Like you

And then…

Me too.

On High

I seen the moon

Rise in the sky.

A quarter moon

It rose on high.

And made the dark

Light in a way.

Tho it was dark

It seemed…

Like…

Day.

There Could Be

There could be no sunrise

If there was no night.

There could be no dark

If there was no light.

There could be no good

If there was no bad.

There would be

Only things

That we thought

We had.

All Around

Little flashes all around
Of lightning in the sky.
While the stars
Are shining bright
In the Heavens high.
Makes the sky
So beautiful
Just
For you and I.
Little flashes
All around
Of lightning…
In the sky.

In The Country

A house in the country
With green trees
All about,
And cows
And things,
With birds on wing.
With quiet too
To just please you,
Seems…
A marvelous thing…
To do.

Four Words

Thank you
And
You're welcome.
Are
Four words to say
That's nice to say.
And helps to make
A beautiful
Day.

Study time

School buses class rooms
Friends there too.
Makes summer time
Study time
Fun time
Too.

In Between

Day time
Night time
Twilight in between.
Casting shadows
With the sunset.
Comes… just before
The dark -
Is seen.

Old Water Pump

Old water pump
Down in the field
Pumpin' water
For the broccoli field.
Makin' the broccoli
Stay nice and green
Just a growin' in the night and day.

Now old Mr. Gopher
He's pretty smart.
Stays in the ground
When the sun gets hot.
And eats what he wants of the broccoli.
In the mornin'
Or the cool of the day.

But the birds
In the air
They really don't care.
Cause…
When they eat broccoli
Ve-ry rarely
Do they share.
In the morning or the cool
Of the day.
Gophers and birds
Just a cheatin' and eatin'
And a havin' their way.
While the water pump watches
And the water pump sees.

continued

Everything from birds to bees
While its down in the field.
Just a pumpin' water.
Co-oo-l
Clear water
Water for the broccoli field.

Yesterday and Today

Yesterday,
Tho past, dull, faded and distant,
Appears,
Artificially bright,
Today,
Stands, present, bright, gleams,
Is near, real and right,
Never,
Return to yesterday,
For,
What yesterday has cast away,
Was,
Used,.
To form,
And to make,
"Today"

Old Clock

Old clock on the wall
Just tickin' away
Tell the time
Of another day.
Twenty four hours
To use as you choose.
Twenty four hours
Of what to say.
Old clock on the wall
Tickin' hours away.

Past Midnight

About one half hour
Past midnight
From behind a mountain nearby.
An orange half moon
Rose silent…
In the deep blue
Star studded sky.
Speaking beautifully different
To all.
Who seen it
Slow- - ly rise…
To blend
With the stars
In the heavens.
And glow
In the star filled
Skies.

So Very Small

Babies are so very small
And sweet as they can be.
They coo and cry
And seldom lie
In places they should be.
Their eyes they move
And look to see.
If things are where
They're heard to be.
If not...
They move themselves around.
And go to where
They want to be.
Oh babies are so very small
But really make fun
For us all.

The Snows

The snows on the mountaintops
Next to the sky.
Mixed with clouds
Hanging low…
Under blue
Heavenly skies.
Reflect soft…
Silent beauty
While ages,
Pass by.

Little Rays

Little rays of sunshine
Say so very much
With their magic fingers
With their magic touch.
Tho they speak to no one,
Yet…
In their special way.
They spread love and sunshine
Every precious day.

Haze Blue

Strange birds flittering twixt
Tall pines
Flowing with the wind.
A lonesome cable car
Ascending
Descending
The mountainside.
With emerald blue waters
Of a lovely lake
In the background.
Blending
With hazy blue.
That stretches
From the waters
To the mountains
To the blue
Of the sky.
Form a heavenly valley
A beautiful scene.

The Blue Jays

The noisy blue jays
In the trees.
Among the needles
And the leaves.
Make noises
That they like to hear.
Awakening every
Listening ear.

The Wind #1

The rushing wind
Among the pines.
Blows dust
And needles.
"Roars"
At times.
And then
It's quiet as can be.
And whispers
Just…
To you
And me.

Understanding

The understanding of the ages

Comes to few

From far.

And yet it seems

The light that's seen

Comes far beyond the stars.

Sent to us

In a spiritual way.

Displayed from day

To endless day.

Felt by many

Felt by few

In steps

That silently slip thru.

In a spiritual way

That's beautiful

As...

The light of day.

A Quiet Road

A quiet road with rambling bush

And tall trees

Stretched

Toward the sky.

Shaded over here and there

As shadows

Follow the sun.

Invites you and I

To amble along

Under a country blue

Heavenly

Open sky.

And feel free as the birds

And a passing bee.

Or a beautiful

Free flying

Butterfly.

Clouds

The sky grew dark
The wind arose
We waited
For the rain.
Then clouds
They parted,
In the sky.
And light…
Shined round
Again.

A Love

The sky is big
The ocean is wide
But people travel
From side to side.
To be with friends
And see with friends
A kind of love
That never ends.

Just Beautiful

Isn't it just beautiful
And a lovely
Sunny day.
When the sun
Is shining brightly
And every thing's
Ok.

Changed

The world is changing everyday
You and I included.
By seconds
Minutes
Hours
Too.
Till when the cycles
Thru.
Everything's
Changed in a way.
It's helping
Start
A new.

All Way Thru

To love all people

And love all things

For the smallest

Things

That they may do.

And not just

Things

We want them to.

Is the only way

That life

Has meaning.

All…

Way…

Thru.

One Way

Oh
Handicaps
We all have them.
In one way
Or
The other.
And that is why
That we should try.
To help
Ourselves
And…
Others.

Night Is Near

Mountains clothed
In reddish haze
Sunsets came
To close the day.
Twilights here
Night is near,
With dark…
To stay
Till day
Appears.

The Mountains

A view of the mountains

I see to the top.

Where they touch

The blue

Of the sky.

Where the sunshine

Seems bright

And glows

In a light.

That fills the world…

With

Shadows

Love…

And delight.

A Shadow

All things I see
It seems to me
Makes a shadow
Beautifully.

Love To All

One light
In the dark
Is like a star.
With love to all
Thru distance
Far.

Auto's Passing

From the window
I see…
Auto's passing in the night.
Silently they come and go.
Where they come from
Where they go.
Only night
And others know.

Seasons

Spring brings rains

And flowers

And things.

Summer

Vacations and trips.

Fall brings Halloween

Thanksgiving too.

Winter brings Christmas

And when it's thru…

A new year comes

For you and me too.

Oh…

Just see what the seasons bring.

Wonderful

Wonderful

Wonderful things.

Around Me

All around me here today
The sky is softly blue.
And over the hills
That's far away
The sky
I'm sure
Is blue today.

The Hillside

There's shadows on the hillside
And sunshine too.
The clouds are very near
And then the sun - shines thru -
Coming this way
To make a nice day.

A Mirror

Everybody's like a mirror,
In all we see and do.
You see you
And others see too.

Hours

Long the sunlight hours
That brighten up the day
And cause the twilight hours
To flow in a magical way.
Making each day special
Like stars in a deep blue sky
Like birthdays that come - pass by.
Hope your birthday was happy

Spent with loved ones
And beautifully enlightening.
As rainbows
As springtime
As...
Your time.

The Wind

Right before the storm goes thru
Is when the wind just howls the most.
Roaring round the house corners
Over window sills
Right across the housetops
Really really shrill,
Like a banshee, calling -
Calling - to you.
But I like the wind
And I like the storms
And I like the puddles
Where the frogs stay warm.
And tho you cannot see the wind
As the storms come thru…
Maybe it comes -
Looking just…
For you –oo
Wh-oo, wh-oo.

The Milky Way

Scattered among the stars so high
Silvery white in the dark blue sky
The Milky Way dwells
Beautifully, majestic…
Over you and I.

Of

Of the evening
What can I say - it closes the day

Of the morning
What can I say - it opens the day

Of noon
What can I say - it's between the night and day

Of the night
What can I say - it has mysterious light,
Light is love
And the love, is of…
Morning, noon, evening, night
Is soft - lovely light.

Stories

For every story

There's another story

That makes it all wrong

To believe what was just said.

And this story

Will prove that is so,

So on and on stories go.

Much like the white

In new fallen snow

Or - the wind that continues to blow. -

For every story

There's another story

Because - people like stories.

And stories,

And stories.

Hey Mr. Janitor

Swing that broom
Flop that mop
Swish swish swish
Flop flop flop
Sweep-a here
Sweep-a there
Push-a push-a
Sweep sweep
Mop-a mop-a
Flop flop
Hey Mr. Janitor
Hey Mr. Janitor
Sweep-ee sweep-ee
Sweepin' -
Sweepin' with your broom
Hey Mr. Janitor
Flop flop.

Christmas

Christmas day is the way
You see the sky
With its blue
Way way up high.
The green of grass
Where people pass.
And deep inside
Where things can hide
Good and bad
There's always…
Waiting just for you
To see it thru.

———————————-

A very merry Christmas
And a holiday season
With the warmest of love
For you and
Those you love.

The Forgotten Folks

Hey over there

You with your heads

Down low.

What makes you so special

To think you know

It can't be

The way it was.

To see the sunshine,

Its always there,

Just covered

By clouds

Sometime.

And you... folks,,,

Way over there

With your head

Down low - thinking' you're forgotten -

Will miss

A nice day

In the sunshine

Because, clouds don't stay.

Hey over there -

continued

Do you hear what I say?

Have a nice day…

With love.

Airports

I like to go to airports

People everywhere I see

Going coming

Here and there

Oh, so happy

It seems to me

But they're

All so very busy

And maybe

What's to see

Is what was there

And what's to be

And what's between

Is for

You and me

To see.

Peanuts

Crush em'
Open em'
Munch on em' too,
Peanuts are really good
For you.
Help yourself
And in this way.
Have a most lovely
Munchin' peanut day
And have it…
Your way.

An April Day

April winds
April sunshine
April blue of sky
With waving grass
Tree braches too
An April day
Just passing thru.

Roses

Oh say

Did you hear the flowers?

The way they bloomed today

It seemed the blossoms waved

And very softy

They did say.

The roses will bloom today

The roses will bloom today

The yellow roses

The red roses

The pink roses

All the roses

Will bloom today.

And the roses all the roses bloomed

And the fragrance of the roses

Filled the air

Of spring sweet - beyond compare

Oh say, did you hear the flowers?

"Did" you hear the flowers?

When they bloomed.

The way they bloomed

Today.

Passing

July is nearly finished
Bringing August very near
Summer is rapidly passing by
As clouds drift in the sky.
When September brings the autumn
And leaves begin to fall
I'll think of June, July, and August
With summer breezes.
Holidays, green of leaves, and all
Then…
When the leaves begin to fall.

Faith

The highest branch - upon a tree

Is where you see the branch to be

And the highest star, that's in the sky

Is where you see it - in your eye

And the light of heart felt love - that shines

From deep within - is how you feel

In your heart - after love comes in.

May you forever feel, wherever you may go

As a beautiful rainbow

Spreading, filling, heavenly, love and faith

Over trees under heavens, under stars

In God's spacious lovely Earth and sky above.

Golden Streak

A golden streak up in the sky

A shooting star

Is passing by.

So fast the star

Does fly on high.

It's gone…

Before I blink

My eye.

Blossoms

Today is the 21st day of March

Just another day

But the first day of spring

Another season

For lovely things

To come forth in - lovely ways.

For the land brings forth

Blossoms at this time

Which chimes in - eternal ways.

That flower forever

To everyone—spiritually

Thru love, and…

In love.

Religious

Religious Index

To All

The homeless on the streets
We meet -
Have little to cover
Their bodies their feet
Except what they carry
That we see.
And it is lovely and also
Eternal -
That we share
Some we have
With them of love
Thru love.
The creations desire
Of love to all
Thru light - thru darkness
In love.

Religious

Something Lovely

Love is something lovely
That bonds -
As clouds to blue sky.
Memory is beautiful too
But fades sometime -
As storms pass thru.
But love is there
As ages pass by
And remains always -
As clouds… to blue sky.

To Have People

More people to help others
Like sisters and brothers
Is what is needed
Each day.
It would brighten like sunshine
Along the way.
Of course… good rules exist -
But others helping others,
Like good sisters and brothers
Would help to make life
More lovely
Like most lovely
Of love.

A Bell

From the gentle ringing

Of a bell

This pleasing sound made

Can tell

Especially at Christmas time

Everyone

Far and near - that…

It's almost Christmas

Will soon be here

Merry Christmas

Merry Christmas

And -

Happy New Year.

The Crucifixion

Who's that a walkin' so slow carryin' his own cross
Why's he a walkin' look now Simon's carryin' his cross
That's Jesus carryin' the sins of the world
That's Jesus carryin' the sins of the world.

Look they are goin' to the place of the skull
Why are they goin' to the place of the skull
Jesus is goin to be hung on his own cross
Jesus is goin' to die on his own cross.

Jesus will be dyin' for the sins of the world
Jesus will be dyin' for the sins of the world
Love came for all now when he died on the cross
Love came for all now when he died on the cross.

Joseph is a goin' and a takin' Jesus' body
Joseph is a putting' Jesus' body in his tomb
Early Sunday morning Mary came to see the body
But Jesus has risen he arose from the tomb.

Chorus
Jesus came from his home on high
Jesus came to this world to die
And no matter what men did to him
He'll return oh he'll come back again.

The Ways Of God

Chorus
Sometimes you can feel the spirit of God reaching' out
Sometimes you can feel the spirit of God reaching' out
For the ways of God are way beyond man's comprehension.
For the ways that God can be wear are beyond man's comprehension

Sometimes when it's quiet and you're al alone
Sometimes when it's quiet and you're al alone
Did you ever feel someone was there with you
Oh the ways of God are way beyond man's comprehension.

If you feel you have done your brother wrong
If you feel you have done your brother wrong
Get on your knees and ask God for forgiveness
Oh the ways of God are way beyond man's comprehension.

If you feel confused and don't know who to turn to
If you feel confused and don't know who to turn to
Pray to God for guidance and his help
For the ways of God are way beyond man's comprehension.

If you are happy share happiness with others
If you are happy share happiness with others
Pray to God for guidance at all times
Oh the ways of God are beyond man's comprehension.
Repeat Chorus

Ruth

Ruth was a lady from the moabite land
She married her husband on God's command
They lived happy in the Moabite land
Till God called Ruth's husband to his heavenly home.

After Ruth's husband had passed away
Ruth went to Bethlehem with Naomi to stay
She gleaned barley in the field each day
Till Boaz seen her working and took notice of her.

Boaz asked about the lady in the field
And learned that she came from the Moabite land
Her husband had died and left her alone
She made her living by gleaning the field.

Boaz thought and watched the lady in the field
Found out her name and fell in love with her
They were married at a time on God's command
And lived with their son Obed in Bethlehem.

Chorus
Ruth, Ruth, God loves you
God's spirit glows in you
Ruth, Ruth, love's in you
Love really shines in you.

Love

What is love, what is love
I ask you, what is love
Oh it comes, from God above
What is love, what is love.

Oh to me, love is free
Comes from God, down to me
But to you, is love free
What is love, please tell me.

In this world, love seems far
Love seems far, on a star
But God loves, you and me
And love's there, and it's free.

If you love, and it's true
You love God, God loves you
We know God, he is true
Love is there, love for you.

Chorus
Oh, love is faith and love is hope
Love is trust and love is care
And It comes from God above
When God sends eternal love.

Of Love

Love is sometimes silent

As the stars above

Yet it is near

Both night and day.

Like moonlight soft

Like sunlight of day.

In memories…

As fields of flowers.

And the beautiful fragrance

Of love…

Is comforting,

Spiritual - eternal,

And…

Flows thru the hours -

Of forever.

Faith

In the sunny days of early spring
And the gentle breezes too.
There's a something…
That seems to rustle blossoms
And helps them - to peep thru.
It's also in soft summer nights
In lengthy winter days
In troubles and in sorrows
In happiness - along life's way.
For it is the love of God
Thru faith, that reaches out
Surrounds, embraces fully
As the mountains…
Round about.

Manipulate

God don't manipulate - this I know
God lets you go - where you want to go
Be it a mountain oh so tall
Or an ocean deep… deep and wide
Wherever you go this I know
God don't manipulate
Is at your side
Loves you - always with you - forgive you
And lets you go
Whenever
Whenever
You want to go.

Stayed

We stayed in a room
In a bed over the spot
Where our son
Had passed thru.
We were happy - in a way
But a tear…
Was passed too - that day.

Comforting Love

So beautiful

And awesome too

Are the flowers

In the fields afar

As they wave - in the wind

Unseen

Neath far off stars

In the heavens.

Thus we behold - that beauty

Surrounds… in abundance

Free.

And the birds, animals, nature

That roam - trusting

Also - but sure… of a love

That cares - for all.

Thru storms, thru calm

Beautiful - lovely

This love is present.

In fields of flowers

Waving in the wind unseen -

In blossoms anew

Continues.....

The snow of winter

The calm of spring

Is near

Always near

Spiritually, lovely, eternal

Thru faith

This comforting love

The Creator's love

Is there for all

Always...and

Forever.

Calling

Above the circle of the Earth

Calling the stars by name

Is God - our God eternal

The same.

Who watches over all

Wherever we go

Whether the pathway

Is bright - or cloudy

Near or far.

God thru faith

Is comforting...

As the stars - in the heaven high

Always near.

Always close by

Through prayer

Through faith

Softly, gently calling

To help.

Love And Faith

The highest branch - upon a tree

Is where you see the branch to be

And the highest star that lights the sky

Is where you see it in your eye

And the light of heartfelt love - that shines

From deep within - is how you feel

In your heart, after love comes in.

May you forever feel

Wherever you go, as a beautiful rainbow

Spreading, filling, heavenly, love and faith

Over trees - under stars - also sunlight

In God's spacious lovely Earth and sky above.

We Behold

Pathways trodden we behold
Each tell a story of youth, of old
From time past - to that of now
And of the family pathways
Formed nurtured loved.
For this love shows
As a beautiful rainbow
Glows in the heavens.
Of love, of care, of devotion
Taught, given, shared,
Creating memories, of and on -
These trodden pathways
That will shine with others - thru others
Together in eternal light…
Forever.

God's Plan

What God planned - and he made plans for you

What God planned that he can do

Eternal life God planned for you

And eternal love he planned that too

All of this and more - God can give to you

Oh yes, what God planned - he can do for you.

All you need is faith - hope and trust

To receive it all.

Trust in God - with faith too

What God planned - it's free for you

What God planned God will do for you

Like the silence of the sunlight

Like the beauty of a rainbow

God's love will shine

Beautiful - radiant

Will shine - will shine in you.

The Ship

The weather was stormy upon the sea
And the ship pitched high and low
While winds out over the sea - over the sea...did blow.
And there was nary a bird
Save an albatross that soared in the sky to see
Where the sunrays crossed - crossed over the sea.
The ship was old, but bold it was
As it fought the stormy sea
It rode the waves, it pitched and rolled
But stayed the course and seen it thru.
Those unseen aboard feared not - because they knew the ship
They knew its silent ways
For it would boast thru groaning movement sounds…
I've sailed before, I'll sail again, I'll sail again, and again
And the ship sailed on into the storms
As the winds blew over the sea.
With nary a soul save the albatross
To see where the ship and the sunrays
Crossed over the sea… while at full sail
The ship, it sailed, forever… forever… and on.

Passes Thru

With the illness of the day
Give us sunshine in your way
To warm as sunrays do
All that they with love shine thru
Of the impossible quite sublime
Give to the Creator of all time.
With the quiet of the night
Give to the soft mysterious… moonlight
In those ways - and in love too
Rage and unrage passes thru.

Saw This

He saw this, my friend told me so
The lamp chain started swinging -
Round and round did go
Making a strong wind as it did go
And a cross did come.
From heaven to Earth, it shined
A cross appeared - from heaven to Earth
And as long.
With Jesus and angels
From heaven to Earth, came down.
Then our fears of all did leave
My friend told me this
And it is so.
For it was told
Told with love -
And it is so.

Ways To Live

You can treat folks good

You can push folks around.

But remember this,

Friend,

What goes up

Must come down,

And

What goes around

Comes around.

So,

Do a little good

Each and every day,

And,

Many good things

Will,

Brighten your day.

The Earthquake #1

The Earth trembled
Buildings shook,
Mountains rolled
The air was still.
God's powers
Were assembled
Speaking to man.
While,
The earthquake
Showed God's power,
By shaking
Man's achievements
And,
The land.

The Earthquake #2

The Earth,
Pitched and rolled
Man trembled.
While, the earthquake,
God assembled.
Shook the land
Reminding man,
God's
In,
Command.

From Afar

The oceans rose

And touched the shores

The sky was dark to see.

And clouds grew dark

The wind it howled

Seemed, everlastingly.

Then trouble brewed

From far away

And came as dark this day.

Some could see

Deep spiritually

The future in that way.

And they grouped and mingled

From a light…

Seen shining from off far

That guided them till sunshine came

With a love…

As deep as the ocean

And beautiful -

As the heaven…

Above.

Starlight

Starlight glowing, oh so bright,
In the heavens, in the night,
High above all,
With your might,
Seeing,
Watching,
Wrong and right,
God gave you,
Dominion, over night,
Starlight,
Starlight,
Oh,
So,
"Bright."

An Experience

To pray is a beautiful experience
Lovely as the dawn
Sunlight, moon, stars at night
It enlightens as vastness
Of waters on the Earth
Prayer gives oneness like
birds that soar in skies
Of blue near the heavens - of love
To pray yields a closeness
With the Creator of all
That patiently waits for our call
And provides help to our words
Many or few.
With the Holy Spirit giving—always
Giving a new, meaning - that -
Praying is a most…
Beautiful experience.

To See

How do I see - the blue of the sky
How do I see the sun so high
How do I see a drifting cloud
Do I see them crowding beauty
Way up high?
How do I see the trees
And the grass so green.
Do I see it all, as a lovely scene
To make the surrounding love
Just musically in tune,
And in step with it all.
This way it becomes, also is
The beauty of an eternal
Beautiful gift, given freely
Everyday in love.
Helping to make lovely
And beautify everything
We behold... wondrously.

Each Given Day

Think of the whole
Of each given day
As it comes to each
In a most beautiful way.
As it gives to all
While hours pass by
Love as silent - like birds that fly.
While light and darkness too
Shine on each
As hours pass thru.
Then eventide comes
A moon climbs in heavens
Stars twinkle ancient
Given lovely too…
Saying it is well
Thru an eternal display
For each with love
Every given day.

This Christmas

The Christmas season of years gone by
Filled the heart with Christmas joy.
And the mountains sang and the hills rejoiced
For Christmas is a season
Of individual choice
As the glow of moonlight
Twilight too
Whispers soft
To a special few.
May this Christmas in a beautiful way

_____

Be filled with love and light
For your loved ones and you
With a meaning special
As skies are blue.

The Wind And Sunshine

The wind sweeps the clouds,
Out of the sky
And sunshine comes.
From God on high
Lights the Earth
For man,
To do good by.

Bits And Pieces

Bits and pieces,
Bits and pieces,
Put together, "good,"
Can,
Be understood,
Bits and pieces,
Bits and pieces.
Put together wrong,
Make trouble,
All day,
Long.

Little Grains

Little grains of rice
Holds the sunshine
And the wind
And rain
And dew.
Little grains of rice
Holds love and life
That God
Gives folks.
Like me
And you.

The Wind

When the wind

Just howls

And the snow

Is deep.

Where the grass

Was green

But is now

Asleep.

Oh it's good to know

God's love

Does flow

To all

Who believe

As the wind…

That blows.

Tones

The strains of music
All played with care
Was written
By the writer
With patience
And care.
Then passed along
With the breeze
As a song.
And the life we live
Is…
But a song.
Written by us
As each day
Moves along.
In words
That's clear
In tones
That's strong.
And played
Thru our lives
As our…

Continues.....

Special

Song,

Then after

We…

Have passed away

To another

Realm.

And endless days

Go an

And on.

This song

Will be known

As ages

Pass by.

As a song

Of life

Another…

Lived

By.

A Meaning

Each day has a meaning
As it comes and goes
Unknown to many
For very few know.
That each day has love
From morning till night.
And glows in its own
Shimmering light.
To be found.
If one listens
Close and adheres.
To each thing
No matter
What size
It appears.
It's filled
With a love
That glows from within.
For this is where
True love
Must come
Deep...

Continues.....

With in.

When this love

We can see

In things

Day by day.

A new dimension

Of life

Comes to stay.

And unknown

To many

But known to a few.

Beautiful love

Then comes shining

Each day…

Right

To you.

The Garden

There is a garden

A garden

Of love.

Warmed by the sun

That shines

From above.

The flowers

That grow

In this garden

Of love.

Get strength

And are healed

By the light.

A heavenly

Light.

A spiritual

Light.

That shines

From above

Continuously…

On all

Continues.....

Who ask.

And truly

Believe.

In God's

Beautiful

Beautiful

Garden.

The garden…

Of,

Love.

A Shadow

All things I see

It seems to me

Makes a shadow

Beautifully.

The Dark

To go beyond

The shadows

Into the dark of night.

And there to light

A candle

Expelling dark.

From light

Gives life

Thru light

And love

In night.

That lives

While there is light.

And when the life

Is lost

To dark

The love that

Was expelled.

Will live

On and on

By those who seen

The life…

Thru light

In dark.

A Love

The waves of the ocean

Gently caress

Seashores

Of the here

And the far…

Far away.

While the leaves

Stir the quiet

Of lonely hours

Just…

Before the onset

Of day.

When the known

And the unknown

Are made known

In a way

As God makes light…

Thru the dark.

That's brilliant thru the fog

As the mist

On the seashores.

Tho quiet as leaves

Continues.....

On the trees.

And spiritually guides

In a heavenly way.

With a love…

That

Never…

Leaves.

Night Is Near

Mountains clothed

In reddish haze

Sunsets came

To close the day.

Twilight's here

Night is near.

With dark…

To stay

Till day

Appears.

It Seems

To behold

The rising and setting

Of the sun.

The silken beauty of twilight

The mysterious heavenly quiet

Of a climbing

Glowing

Full moon.

Is beauty

And wonders

Of God.

Just for us…

As we mingle

And pass

Briefly…

Amid God's love

Thru life

While life…

Lasts.

In this beautiful

Spiritual

Continues.....

And wonderful

Realm.

Where it seems

There is always

A guiding light.

Thru the shadows

To the valleys beyond

Which glows forever.

With an abundance

Of love.

Beautiful

Spiritual

Eternal

Heavenly…

Love.

A Mother's Love

As morning sun

Shines in the sky.

Heralding

A bright

New day…

On high.

Somewhere

A little baby

Softly cries.

A brand new life

A mother's love

Has just begun.

A love that is

The only kind.

Tho one may search

Thru endless time.

Then look inside

And finally find.

A mother's love

As love from God.

A love that lasts

Continues.....

Tho ages pass.

A mother's love

As light of day

Goes…

On

And on.

Light - Dark

Light is light

Whenever light is -

For light is light.

And…

Dark is not -

There is no dark.

For dark is where,

There is no light.

Beauty Forever

The beauty of a snow storm

Is there to see

When we can see

The beauty

Of the wind

The Earth

And the snow.

Together.

The beauty of a rainbow

Is when we see

The colors

The heavens

The calm

The love

Altogether.

The beauty of each other

Is the love

We can see

The love

We can feel

The love that

Continues.....

44 Religous

Is known

To each other.

The beauty of love

Is what we share

The quiet

The care

The presence of each other.

For

The beauty

Of the

Snow

The beauty

Of the wind

The beauty of

Of the Earth

The beauty

Of a rainbow

Is spiritual.

True love

For each other

Is also

Spiritual.

Continues.....

And remains

Forever.

Is

Eternal

For God is love

And if love

Is true

It is of God

It is beautiful

It is

Forever.

Little Bird

Little bird in the sky,

Close to heaven as you fly,

Watching man pass below,

You,

So high,

He,

So low.

The Winds

The winds of march

Caress my face

And I feel their

Soft embrace.

And the mountains

I see

Surrounding me.

Tho they utter

Not a word.

Their presence is felt

And I am not

Alone.

The love they send

Is forever near.

Tho the winds travel on and on

And

The mountains may crumble

To dust.

The love they've sent

Thru the lives

They touched.

Continues.....

As the love

Of those

We've known.

Will be felt

Forever and on.

In a very special way.

That will glow

With a spiritual

Heavenly light.

Forever…

In an

Eternal

Way.

The Ocean

My friend the ocean

Said to me.

Come with me

And see what I see.

Just stand upon

My quiet shores.

And mix your thoughts

Within my waves.

Then let them go

And just explore

With my waves.

As…

My waves

Travel

From shore

To shore.

If this you do

When you feel inclined

Come to my shores

From within your mind.

And let your thoughts

Continues.....

So entwine

With my waves

As they travel

Under God's open sky.

That love and light

May enter your life.

Letting universal vibrations

Guide your way.

And you can then

Have a happy

Heavenly

Spiritual

Day.

Tell Them

Tell them of the burning bush.

And of the staff

That turned to snake

Then…

Back to staff

Again.

"Tell them"

Of that…

"Also"

Tell them of the withered hand

Restored to whole again.

Tell them of the miracles

Performed for love of man.

Tell them that I watch

As men go

From day to day.

That I watch

How they treat others.

And the things

They do…

And say.

Continues.....

Tell them I reward…

Rebuke…

And that I

Chastise too.

But…

Tell them…

That I do

This all

For love.

Because

"I," am "Am"

"JEHOVAH"…

The one who created

Heaven, Earth

And all.

"That"…

Is who

I," am "Am"

"Tell them"

Please…

"Go"

"Tell them."

To Venture

To venture forth
With the wings of the dawn.
And hear a bird sing
Its beautiful song.
To venture forth
On the ocean wide
And command the unknown
With the world
At your side.
Then
To sail
Thru the deep
To a port of your own.
Where a golden tomorrow
Awaits you alone.
Is a venture of love
And accomplishment too.
In the follow
Of a light…
That only
You can see…
Thru.

Build

Build a rocket

And a plane.

Build equipment

Harvest grain.

Build a ship and travel the Earth.

Build a telescope

Study the stars.

And see far-rr beyond

Where distant galaxies are.

Then study the body…

The body of men.

That marvelous temple

We dwell in.

The temple of God.

And few…

If any

Will disagree.

There's much

For men

To study

And understand.

Continues.....

To realize
"Only partially."
The marvelous
Mysterious
Spiritual
Structure,
Of man.

Folded

I seen the flag tucked
And folded away
With 3 stars showing
In such a way
A triangular fashion
Was made.
It spoke not a word
But said many things
Of honor
Thru silence
To someone…
The flag brings.

An Inner Strength

Deep

Deep inside

Where no one

Can see.

There's

A spiritual

Inner strength…

That really

Helps me.

I go

De-ep

Inside

When I

Really want to.

And get

Loving help

That's beautiful…

And

True.

To You

Who can say

Where the thrust sword

Falls.

Who can say

Where all

Rain

Drops fall.

Who can say

Where the wind will blow…

This

Very day.

But it matters not…

What others say

For love is here

It's here to stay.

And if you listen

Quiet and true.

True, love

Will say

All…

Things…

To you.

Those We Meet

The winds blew soft

In silence…

Tho they spoke,

But yet

We knew

That they were there.

Thru flut-tering

Of the leaves

And shapes of limbs

Upon the trees.

The ocean waves

Drift quietly by

And yet we know

The winds are nigh.

And help shape shorelines

Of the world

As time flows by.

Those we meet

Like wind and waves

Shape our lives

In special ways.

Continues.....

And when they leave

Their spiritual presence

Is forever

Felt

Thru memories…

That are beautiful

As the heavenly winds

And ocean waves,

And ever present

In loving

Spiritual

Ways.

One Highway

The many paths we travel

That lead to one highway

The ones we meet

Along the way,

The ones that start us

On the way.

They shine as stars

In heaven high

And when a star

Falls from the sky

It leaves a void

And marks the sky.

But memory of the star

On high

Will light the dark

A special way

And spiritually guide

The loved along,

The one highway

They travel on.

Love

If you love
There is no fear.
And if you fear
There is
No love.
For true love…
Rules…
The very heart
And knows…
Only love
Only love
Only love.

Shade

The shade of a tree - that offers the sun

A place for a shadow to form.

To shelter a growing love - that grows to love the tree

That loves the sun.

And then grows to places of love - love of another

Like a child to adult - a wife -

Children - father mother.

Thru storms, rainbows - clear skies - sunny weather

Also a place where children grow

Where life is fun for everyone.

A place where age is born

And a place where if a call from far away

Calls one away - a love remains

A memory too that grew

From the shade of a living tree,

That grew from the love of a heavenly son

That gave lasting -

Eternal spiritual light, and love

For everyone.

A Sunset

With golden hue a sunset lovely
Paints an evening sky
And with love the mornings sunrise
Golden sunrise...
Lights crystal, blue of sky.
While in the time that's - in between
Flowers bloom - flowers grow.
Trees from seedlings fully grow.
Children, families, bloom and grow
And in the waters - life there too -
View the sun, moon... passing thru.
When comes the dark - near twilight time
A firefly dances, disappears - then reappears
Creating memories, like harvest...
While with golden hue a sunset lovely
Paints an evening sky.
And with each mornings sunrise
Golden sunrays memorably
Lights - crystal blue of sky.

Each Given Day

Think of the whole
Of each given day
As it comes to each
In a most beautiful way
As it gives to all
While hours pass by
Love as silent
Like birds that fly.
While light and darkness too
Shines on each
As hours pass thru
Then even tide comes
A moon climbs in heavens
Stars twinkle ancient
Given all lovely too… saying it is well.
Thru an eternal display
For each with love…
Every, given day.

For Everything

A time a place for everything
It seems that's what's written to be
For everything that's all about
From the shores to the shining seas.
Even the children that sing and play
Then learn as they see, as they play
The teachers that teach
The leaders that lead
The buildings that came
The materials too, designed
To tell what to do.
All have a way to be, to stay
To fill a planned spot
In the maze of days
That pass continuously on
In a time a place for everything
It seems... that's what's written to be.

Thru Love

To shake a tree
When it's filled with green.
And feel vibrations
That's unseen.
To pray when the mind
Is filled with doubt.
Is what the world
Is all about.
To believe the things
We cannot see.
With faith
Thru love
That they, may be.

Set Me Free

I worked for a man
He bridled me
I worked for another
He set me free.
The one I remember
The other…
Was me.

Take Time

Take time
To feel the touch
Of a falling raindrop.
To see the beauty
Of a blade of grass
Or a single flower.
Take time
To feel the race
Of passing hours.
And the flow
Of seconds
Fill…
The vacant hours.
Then…
Take time
In silence
And see.
The love of God
With…
Eternity.

Light

Dark covers the sun

When a storm

Is nigh.

But blue sky

And sunlight

Recover…

Their place

In the sky.

_____

May brilliant light

Shine

On all things

For you.

Recovering

For you,

The things…

You most

Want it too.

A Spiritual Touch

The hills and mountains
Are alive
With green
That comes from the master's touch.
And the blue of the sky
Seems far away
Brightened by the sun
Of a golden
Today.
The love these wonders
Has brought to us
Is enriched
By your marriage today.

May your marriage
Be filled with love
And happiness.
Glowing and lengthy
As the rays
Of the sun.
That shine form the blue
Of the heavens
Far - away.
With a spiritual
Touch.
Of forever
And…
Today.

Each Day

Forgive as the sun forgives-
Clouds that sometime
Hide sky blue on high.
Forgive as green grass, drifting
Autumn leaves that cover-
Green grass till spring.
Forgive as shorelines the waters,
As tides come and go.
Forgive as parents a growing child-
A growing child, the parents…
As life comes—and goes.
Forgiveness is love, that lights
In a way, like sunshine…
Each day.

Far Far Away

From across the ocean

Far far away

You came…

And worshipped God

With us

In our Christian

Way.

In Sunday school

And worship

Service

Too.

May God be with you

And bless each

Of you.

As you leave

To go

Upon

Your way.

And always

Be near you.

In a

Continues.....

Special…

Spiritual…

Eternal…

Way.

Shaded

A loss whenever

It may be

Marks an event

Forever

That can never

Be erased.

It comes forever

To recover

At that special ray

Of shaded

Eternal sunshine.

Acts

Strong

The waves of the ocean

Lengthy

The hours of time

Bright

The light of the sun

Shimmering

The light of he moon

Glowing

The light of the stars

Binding

The chains of a slave

Shameful

The deeds of a wrong

Beautiful

The giving of love

Forgiving

The acceptance of wrong

Amazing

The hands of help

Loving

Continues.....

The acceptance of change

Progress

Living by

The golden rule.

Learn

Love—marriage

Family time

Children too (maybe)

And when they grow

Thru

Family time—too,

Their own.

Then is…

Family time

Of only two-

A special time

To learn again of marriage

And love too.

The Withering Flower

The whispering winds

Knows secrets...

For they've borne the sands of time

Across the centuries.

They've blown where nothing was.

They've blown where civilizations

Rose, flourished and crumbled

Into the dust from whence they came…

And as the winds

That blew from no where

Yet they're felt across

The Earth.

A flower flourishes

Spreading beauty

Spiritual beauty…

That radiates round the Earth.

And continues…

Tho the flower

May wither and fade.

The lasting beauty

That it's made

Will vibrate

Continues.....

Spiritually

On and on.

As the whispering winds

Across the centuries.

And thru the realms

Of forever

And ever…

And on.

Magic

The magic of the sunlight
Drives dark of night away
Uncovering all the mysteries
The dark has laid away.
And quiet of each morning hour
Mixed with sky blue
Far away
Makes light…
The passing cares of day
Thus hours glide
Gradually
Fading away.

May the light of heaven
Eternally smile on you
In all - that you may
Ever do.
Today and everyday
Your entire life…
Thru.

Forever

May the warmth and cheer

That lingers here

Be brightened

By your presence here.

And,

May the brilliance

Of the sunlight

The beauty of a rainbow.

The glow of the moonlight.

And all other heavenly

Love and beauty

That abounds.

Be with you and your family

With God's special spiritual blessings.

Forever

And ever

And ever.

With Love

As the sun rises

Each and every day

It seems so near

Tho far away.

Sending love, warmth

And spiritual cheer

Day by day

Throughout the years.

And as each day

Moves into night.

As birth, life, ages

Take on their flight.

Love reflects love

Tho out of sight.

From those who've been

Within the light.

With love

That's spiritual

In it's own way.

To others

Each and every day.

Continues.....

As God lights all

In his own

Special

Way.

No Fear

I have no fear

When you are near

Beside me, right next to me.

Behind me - or in front

I don't feel the same

I have some fear.

But when you are near me,

There is a love - a spiritual love…

I cannot see - but feel,

And then, I have no fear.

Summer's Gone

Crispy leaves are falling down
Turning pretty golden brown.
Autumn's coming here to stay...
With hazy Indian Summer days.
Bringing harvest with it too,
Pumpkins
Apples
Grapes
And such.
Very good things
For me and you
Summer's gone
But will return
Next year
After early spring,
But now...
Crispy leaves are falling down
Turning pretty
Golden brown.

The Light

Standing majestically tall and serene
The mountains forever and ever
It seems.
Catches the glimpse
Of bright heavens eye.
Reflected in beauty
To both
You and I.
And tho there be darkness
Or tho there be light.
Tho we are troubled
Or burdens are light.
The glimpse of the light
Of bright heaven's eye
Forever shines bright
With a spiritual light.
That shines forever
Encircling all,
With a beautiful
Beautiful
Glow of love.
From God
On high.

Special Ways

I thought I heard the tumble

Of the petals

Of a rose.

But they were cushioned

By the powers

That enable it to grow.

I thought tho skies were dark

And then the sunshine

Came right thru.

With light that

Just encircles ,

And sends comfort

With it too.

May these powers

That sends light

In special ways.

Just encircle

You

And those you love,

In

Spiritual

Heavenly

Ways.

Faith And Love

So beautiful each morning new

That causes us to see

The light of day

Given to us in a way

If we believe - thru

The gifts of love and faith

So beautiful are these gifts

Of faith and love

So eternal in their ways

They help to clear the clouds,

Bring dawn and light…

Of lovely day.

A Child

I'm a child

I learn everyday

Even when I play

From what I see others do

From what I see and do.

From what you think

From what you touch

From how you teach

And what you say

And what I see

And what I see - how I see - what I see

What you think I see

I grow a little someway, everyday

Also I say just what I hear to say

And sometime when I grow big like you

I want to be friends

And say thank you

From a child...

We helped

They helped

The child helped, patience helped

We all... thru.

Thru

Making a complete change
Going the other way
Anytime -
A turnabout,
Spring, summer, autumn,
Winter or fall
Could be…
Disastrous, or -
Lovely, most beautiful,
Too.
By giving another chance
With new faith, love, and understanding
To think it all -
Thru.

In Memory

From blossoms come flowers, beautiful
That travel the Earth like winds.
And the winds together with rainbows lovely
Adorn the Earth.
When a rainbow disappears,
Its love continues on in memory.
And the flower with beauty
Lives on, and on, and for others, on.
Disappearing… tho thru memories, then…
Appearing like flowers, like rainbows.
Leaving - returning seasonal - blossoming lovely -
Making beautiful, eternally lovely…
For the Earth.

Miscellaneous

In Love

So lovely the light of the sun
To start a day
So lovely the light of the moon
To light the night
All to give love
In beautiful ways
That continue eternally all our days.
Love is given in many ways
Your love is so lovely in your marriage.

And continue this love
To each other - to others
As the light of the sun
As the light of the loon
As the light of love
Continues spiritually on…
On and on
In love - lovely
Forever.

The Brightest

Tis when the candle
Burns the brightest
Is when the dark
Is in full light.
And when the sunlight
Is so beautiful
Is when the night
Feels rays of light.
For when dark
Feels love
And light is love
Then love
Covers all
In an eternal way.
As night
Gives way
To light of day.

Highway

My way is the highway
And don't you - even -
Try to change it.
My way is the highway
Everybody just believe
It.
That's the way it's
Gonna be - because -
Nobody's gonna
Change me…
My way is the highway,
"I'm me."

For You

The sky seem so empty
But yet it's filled
With love for things all around.
And a lonesome flower
Is full of love
For the one whom the flowers found.
But this_____ is just filled with love
As the sky and the flower too
For this love is my love
And my love is for… own-ly you.

Marriage

Sultry clouds high in the sky
Drifting passing aimlessly by
Over the motionless, restless sea
That flows… over ancient stone
With living trees
Mid shores
Where waters green
With ocean foam - as white as clouds
On high - do roam.
All this blended, in a beautiful light
That shines in this magnificent sight
Of marriage - twixt the Earth and sky
Is beautiful.
May your marriage

Be filled with beauty
And love
As the marriage - of
The Earth and sky
That tolerates
Much - thru love
As forever
Flows - gently by.

Of Faith

The winds of faith
Blow far and wide
Bringing friends of old
To each other's side
To share of days
The best of days
And birthdays too
Happy birthday

Wishing the best of best
With blessings too
For those you love
And especially for you.

The Sunflower

When dark
Comes each day to stay
And each morning
Goes away
The sunflower
Never turns away
And waits for sunshine
Thru clouds and dark
Till sunshine comes
Somewhere...
Each and everyday.

Cars

I like old cars
That kind of -
Shiver and squirm
Not really too firm
That thump and bump
To let you know
They want to go
Where you like to go.
If a car is, as quiet as
A mouse in its house
Or a bird in the air
I soon feel so, all alone,
Because, I like to hear -
A thump and a bump
To let me know - the car is happy
To go, where, I like to roam.

Friends

I'm your friend
Do you really hear me?
I'm your friend
Do you see me
Do you hear, what I have to say
Do you care, what I have to say
Ask me if you do,
So you can hear me through.
I will do the same for you
Please hear me
I'm your friend.
Will you be my friend too?...
That's what real friends do.

The People

Now listen
Now listen
The people have spoken
Their voices shall now
Be heard.
For they have voted
They've voted
The election's been held
And what they have
Spoken by election,
With ballot - and
Thought - and desire.
Will be victorious - and -
With love beheld.
The people have spoken...
Now listen,
Now listen.

A Beautiful Way

Somewhere over tomorrow
And maybe today,
The sun will shine
In a beautiful way.
Melting the clouds
That cover the sky
Hiding the blue
From you and I.
Somewhere somehow
Near far away
The sunbeams just gather
To make up
Each day.
And the breeze's blow soft
Like the blue in the sky,
Causing each day.
To drift - as a stream,
Flowing by.

So Beautiful

Pay attention to a child
Maybe change
Make its life worthwhile.
Pay attention to the flowers
As the hours
Passeth by
Watch them change
Make beautiful colors
Blossom under
Silent skies.
And their colors
Change with seasons
As the seasons
Passeth by
Changing hours, years with reason
As attention
Blinks an eye.
Then we wonder
And we ponder

continues..........

While we go upon our way,
As attention makes
So beautiful -
Children
Flowers
Seasons
Days.

The Brain

So wonderful the brain
It works in spite of storms
And when the rain
Begins to fall
Or snow begins to blow
The wondrous qualities
Of the brain
Decides what, right
Or left sides
Of the brain
Must tell the body-best-
To know
So wonderful the brain

In The Evening

There's something, in…
The powers of evening
When at - or near
The close of day.
When the sun… drops near the tree line
Is when the silence
Has its say.
Kind of speaks
To cleared minds memories
When the positive
Clears the way
As in spring - a breath of summer
Melts the wintry
All away
Oh there's something
Magic
In the evening - near the trees
At close of day.

On And On

Take time each day
As the sun shines
As the breezes blow
As the dust rises - settles
Moves –.
As the moon, twilight
Shades of evening
Night and stars glow thru.
To never forget
Tho you're away
You thoughts - our thoughts
And our love too
Goes on, and on
As light,
To you.

Sunset In The Mountains

Dropping sun,
Disappearing o'er the mountains,
Lengthening shadows,
Gradually covering,
The valley floors.
Darkness,
Restless sunlight
Early,
In the valley.
Although
The sun still shines bright
On the mountains
At the top.
But,
This is the way of life
Everyday in the mountains.
When,
God's sunshine,
Turns to sunset,
In a day,
Of mountain,
Life.

The Parade

Happy smiling, serious faces,
People walking while music embraces,
Their inner thoughts.
Ever listening for a,
Distant, drumbeat.
To guide their ever moving feet,
And,
Following a guide,
With whom they abide.
To take them safely
Wher'ere he guides.
People marching,
Following,
Mimicking,
In the parade,
Life's,
Parade.

The Joys Of Christmas

The mystery of Christmas
Arrives this time of year.
Spreading its joys of,
Love, hope, faith, charity and cheer.
For many,
It's a joyous time of year.
For others,
It's a very sad time of year.
To watch many blessed,
With family and friends,
Sharing the joys of Christmas,
To no end.
But Christmas is a time
For giving, sharing,
And spreading.
The Holy Spirit,
And,
The Christmas spirit.
So that,
True love,
From,
The depths of our hearts,
Will spread,
And continue,
To spread.
On,
And on,

Continues.....

And on.
To all,
Throughout,
The,
"Earth."

Up With The Sunshine

Up,
With the sunshine,
Far, far,
Above the clouds,
Up,
Where the air,
Is, crisp and clear.
Up,
Where there's, probably no trouble anywhere.
You,
Could, probably see, everything, everywhere.
But,
You could,
Never meet people,
Like,
Your friends,
Or I,
If you stayed,
That high,
In the clear, cold, sky.

Universal Language

The moon,
And,
The stars,
Shine bright tonight.
Lighting,
The Earth,
With a,
Soft glowing light.
That seems,
To speak,
In a soft,
Loving voice.
Saying,
Come,
Rest,
Live quietly.
For,
Love,
Rules,
The night.

Pitter Patter

Pitter patter, children's chatter
Pitter patter in the house.
Tricycles, bicycles, toys all over,
Clutter around, all over the house.
They rush right home
After school is out,
Open their bags
Take their school studies out.
Prepare a light snack,
Study, then run about.
But, when evening is nigh
And dark shadows come.
The children,
Bid friends bye,
And, straight home they come.
To make,
Pitter patter children's chatter,
Pitter patter, in the house.

The Salinas River

The Salinas River, runs underground
And peeps up occasionally
When heavy rains, are around.
Then it,
Flows o'er its banks
And roars savagely on
Till it silently, quietly, slips underground.
There storing its water in caverns,
Under the earth,
Where farmers sink wells,
Deep into the earth.
Pumping water from caverns
Of the river underground.
Keeping Salinas Valley green
Tho the rivers unseen.
But,
The river has a philosophy
All of its own,
It gives life, it takes life,
And, flows on alone.
Till it feeds,
To the ocean,
Mixing with waters,
From all o'er,
The Earth,
Continuing,
Its cycle,
God gave it,
From birth.

Cannery Row

Cannery row,
Happened in old Monterey,
When old Monterey California
Was in its heyday.
When sardine fish came,
In large numbers.
To, the waters of Monterey Bay.
Large canning companies
Were built to can
Sardines that came from
The Monterey Bay.
This area was called
Cannery Row,
With a colorful history
That lives on today,
Tho changes since the sardines have left.
It remains,
Tho somewhat dim,
But, its memories,
Shine on thru
A shimmering haze,
Perhaps,
From another world.
Giving,
Nostalgic memories
Of,

Continues.....

Old Monterey,
And of,
Colorful
Cannery
Row.

Tough Going

When,
The going gets tough
And you've had enough.
Just, get up
Take a little rest,
Then,
Get back in,
Start, with a grin
Finish, the task
Sit back in the sun.
Take a little break,
And reward yourself
With a task,
Well done.

Sometime

Sometime,
I'll take a really
Slow method of transportation,
And move away from civilization,
To a really quiet place
Far, far away from,
The noisy crowds.
Where only me,
And my spirit teacher guide,
Can commune, and take great pride
In the beautiful countryside. Where,
I've decided to take a rest,
From the noisy , boisterous crowd.
I'll stay there, and I'll meditate
For awhile.
Take it real, real easy,
Where it's nice and breezy.
When I feel I'm rested,
Feel I'm ready to return again.
I'll take a real slow method
Of transportation,
Move back to noisy civilization,
And resume my spot in,
Progressive,
Civilization,
Again.

Just Shaved

I just shaved,
So folks can look
And say,
My, his face is clean as can be,
Just like a peach,
See, see.
Then they think,
No,
He's just shaved.
Otherwise his face would be,
Just,
Like the trunk,
Of an old oak tree.
But it still,
Looks like a peach,
To me.
You,
Just take a look,
And see.

The Stars

The stars, tonight
Shine,
Very bright,
And,
Look like candles
In the sky.
Heavenly candles,
In the sky.
Perhaps,
They're beacons
In the heavens.
To guide travelers,
To a land.
That,
We don't remember
Or,
Understand.
But,
The stars,
Shine bright,
Tonight,
Very, very,
Bright,
Tonight.

Moving Ahead

Seems like
Every time
I pick one foot up
The other goes down
And,
I keep moving ahead
Towards
Another town.
I guess it's ok
To move ahead
That way.
Picking,
One foot up
Putting one foot down.
That's one way,
For sure,
To get
Far far
Away
From this town.

A Drop Of Water

A drop if water
Is small,
Very small,
But, if,
A drop of water
Falls everyday,
On a solid rock,
It will wear,
The rock,
Away.

A Passing Cloud #1

A passing cloud,
Dropped rain from the sky.
The rain fell on people,
Both you and I.
That a passing cloud
So high in the sky,
Should think of folks
Like you and I.
Is something,
To remember.
When,
You're nice and dry.

A Passing Cloud #2

A passing cloud,
Dropped rain from the sky.
The rain fell on people,
Both you and I.
That a passing cloud
So high in the sky,
Should drop,
Rain from the heavens.
On you and I.
Is,
A blessing from God.
Who rules,
Earth,
Heaven,
And sky.

Someone To Blame

Isn't it a shame,
Oh,
Isn't it a shame,
That,
Everyone needs,
Someone,
To blame.

I Am Somebody

I may be small,
And,
Not so tall.
But,
I, am somebody.
I, am, me.
No,
One,
Else,
Can see,
As I see.
Walk as I walk,
Talk as I talk
Do what I do.
Or,
Think as I think.
Only me,
So,
Please,
Tell the world,
I,
Am,
Somebody.
Because,
"I,
Am,
Me."

Cub Scout Night

Eyes aglow,
Cub Scouts know,
Tonight's the night
The parents watch,
Their boys,
Put on the show.
Proud parents,
Sitting everywhere.
Just starring,
Wide eyed,
From their chairs.
Course…
The boys,
The boys,
They know.
Tonight's,
The night,
They,
Put on,
The show.

If

If, you could
Raise your hand, and cause the winds
To cease
And blow no more.
If, you could speak
And cause the oceans
To cease
And roar no more.
If, you could sigh
And cause the sun and moon
To fade
And shine no more.
YOU, would have awesome powers
My friend, awe some powers
BUT, from what I understand.
You, cannot even make
A grain of sand.

Different Worlds

We live in different worlds,
You and me,
You,
Live for you,
I,
Live for me.
You,
See the sun
I,
See the moon.
You, see the moon,
I, see the sun.
That way,
Out lives,
Are not the same,
And
Love,
Is only,
Just, a name.
There always,
Appears to be,
One big,
Empty room,
For you and me.
Because,
We live,

Continues.....

In,
Two,
Different,
Worlds

What We Do

It's hard
To cover what we do
The old,
Paths keep shining thru,
And thru,
And thru,
And thru.
Not showing,
Where we're going.
Just showing,
What we've,
Been thru.

Isn't It A Shame

Isn't,
It a shame,
That,
A person,
Can't be,
Exactly,
Where they really want to be.
Drifting,
On a cloud,
Or swinging on a star.
Just, watching Earth turn
Like,
A big candy bar.

The Moon

The moon,
Is high in the sky tonight
The sun,
Is gone, there's no sunlight.
So,
The moon lights night,
The sun lights day.
That,
Brightens each life,
In, a very merry way.

Intermittent Rain #1

It starts to rain,
And then it stops,
Then it rains, real hard again.
It's hard,
To know,
Just what to do.
When the rain,
Plays jokes,
Like this,
On you.

Intermittent Rain #2

It starts to rain,
Then,
It stops,
And then,
It starts to rain again.
It's hard, to know,
Just,
What to do.
If,
The rain,
Don't fall,
Right down,
On you.

Sunrise And Sunset

The sun rises in the morning
Without any warning
And sets in the very
Late evening.
But just before sunset,
And,
A little before moon rise,
The sun saves a little light. (twilight)
So,
The moon can see,
To
Rise just right.
Then,
The sun sets in,
The very late evening,
Without any warning,
As,
It rose,
Early in the morning.

Time

The morning came,
And, passed away,
Noon time came,
In a normal way.
But twilight,
Waited,
Till the time,
Was right,
Painting the world,
With colors,
Of light.
Then,
Night slipped in,
When,
The time,
Was,
Just right.
And,
Covered the world
With,
Glowing,
Moon light.

Traveling

Traveling in the sky,
With the birds,
Sun, moon, and stars.
Man,
Travels high, and far.
Falling sometime,
Climbing with time.
Man,
With the help,
Of,
Machines and things.
Travels high,
And,
Far in the sky.

The Trip Is Over

The trip is over
The waiting is done.
And now,
Beautiful things,
Can be done.
The trip is over,
The traveler,
Is home.

Just Chatting

Sitting, chatting,
Drinking tea,
And,
Passing time away.
Things pass easily
Quietly,
Any hour of the day.
When people,
Sit, chat, drink tea,
And,
Pass the time, away.

Crossing Paths And Time

Isn't it strange
We've lived so close
And, been so near.
But,
Our paths never crossed
Until this year.
With crossing paths
And
Passing time
Friendship in this world
Will surely climb.
But,
Isn't it strange,
How things change,
With time,
With time.

Moon Glow

Moon glow,
After the sunset
Where the air,
Is clear and free.
When the day time
Noise,
Is hushed,
And the nightlife
Is brave and free.
Life,
Takes on added meaning,
In the moon glow,
After the sunset.
When the air is clear,
Life is free,
And,
The moon,
Glows,
Silently.

The Airplane

Soaring high in the sky
Drifting above the clouds
Where the sun is bright.
The airplane floats,
Quiet as can be,
High in the sky,
Where the air is free.
With only the sun,
And the heavens,
Between it,
And,
Eternity.

Evening In The Sky

Long shadows in the sky
Ebbing sunlight in the sky.
Twilight quietly enters in,
Paints the sky where it has been.
Long shadows,
Ebbing sunlight.
Make,
Sunset and twilight,
In,
The sky.

The Mountains And Sky

The mountains are high,
Very near the sky,
Tall and serene,
And make,
A beautiful scene,
The mountains, and sky.
So ancient,
And high,
Looking down,
From above.
On you,
And I.

Moonlight Tonight

The moon's not full
But it's pretty tonight
Way up in the sky
All yellow and bright.
Surrounded by stars
With few clouds in sight.
Its soft... nice to see
The moonlight, tonight.

When I See

When,
I see a small baby,
I see,
Love, care, trust,
When,
I see a small child,
I see,
Love, care, trust,
When,
I see,
Love and care.
When, I see a young adult,
I see,
Love and care.
When I see two lovers,
I see,
Blind love, and care.
When I see marriage
I see,
Love, sometimes,
Care, sometimes,
Trust, sometime.
When,
I see,
An aged person,
I see,
Memories,
Reminiscence,
Yesterday.

A Shower

To take a shower
And feel fresh as a flower,
At the end of the day.
Is like floating on clouds
In an odd,
Kind of way.
But, is quiet refreshing,
At the end,
Of the day.

Following You

The steps you make,
Confuse,
Me at times.
So,
I must make,
My own way through.
Because,
I have lost step,
Following,
You.

A Home And A House

A home is a place
Where you want to be
Hate is there,
Bu love is free.
You can take off your shoes,
And take a snooze,
Wherever you want,
Whenever, you choose.
A house is a place,
That's polished,
Like glass,
And you're afraid to touch things,
They may break as you pass.
Where hate and love
Don't come from above.
So, a home is the place,
I'd rather be,
And, I'm sure there's others
That, think like me.

Our Cars

Cars, cars, cars,
My, how they behave.
A large part of our lives,
From birth to the grave.
Anything they crave,
We get,
We're their slaves.
Cars, cars, cars,
My,
How they behave.

Old Cars

A penny, a dime,
Dollars sometimes,
Hope a little,
Push a little,
Pray a little,
Give of your time.
Old cars,
Love,
Pennies, dimes, dollars,
Prayers, hope,
And push,
Sometime.

An Old House

An old house,
Sagging with age,
Filled with memories
From,
Another age.
In the living room,
A broken dish,
A rocking chair.
In, the bedroom
A feather mattress,
A cane bottom chair,
An old rag doll,
On the bedroom floor.
Just,
An old house,
But,
Rich in memories.
Of...
Another
Age.

To Share

There's a meaning in this season
That shines thru to everywhere
Tho it's understanding
Is quite different
To many - far and near.
And the beauty - is as clouds
That cover the sun, and moon, so high
Lost and wandering - in a jungle
Tho love is near, to you and I.
And the many thru this season
Happy as it seems to be
Happy as it is to see
For birth and love
Just flow as rivers
Moved with love - and spirituality
But some wait, and wait, and wait -
Wait continually...
For the meaning of this season
That shines thru to everywhere
Past, now, many - as,
A cross of love
For all...
To share.

And Then

Storms come first - and then the rainbow
Darkness first - and then light
Morning - noon - twilight - evening
Then soft glow
Of moon at night.
The cross that stands and marks a summit
As the sun so very high
Or a load or heavy burden
Carried
Marks a traveler nigh.
Traveling - traveling
As the sunshine - warms a seed
From inner - thru
To grow beautiful
Mysterious - lovely
As the realm - it passes thru.
Tho storms come first
And then the rainbows
Spiritual light…
Shines bright
Guides thru.

To All

In appreciation
For the seconds of the day
For the hours - months - the years
For the ocean waves so bright
Capped with white
In bright sunlight.
For the mountains oh so tall
From grains of sand
So very small
For the shorelines stretched so far
Neath the beauty of the stars.
From the mountains
In a way
Washed quiet silent day by day.
From the springtime - thru the fall
Leaves that drift - seeds that fall
Seeds that blossom - mysteriously
Living wondrous beautifully
Cycling - recycling, as the seasons.
In appreciation - for this love
Gifts both great and gifts of all
From the master of love to all.
Thanks is given - in a way
Thru light - thru love
Thru appreciation
Thru dedication

Continues.....

Individually
From all…
Day
By day.

A Perfect Way

The way to start
Each given day
Is look to the sky
And see the rainbow
If there's been a storm.
Or distant cloud - or clear sky
Is a lovely place to try.
Also with the Creator's help
Thru the gift of prayer
The Creator can help
Guide us each day

_____

With a perfect way
The start and live
With love
Every given day.

The Petals

Silent as whispers the petals fell
From the flower once beautiful to see
That grew from a seed
Among grains of sand
Lonesome and dark
Where darkness be.
But life so beautiful
With in the seed
Blossomed forth
From dark to light above
And grew to a flower
With abundant love
To share in a beautiful way
In dark and in light of day
Tho now…
As petals fall silent
The beauty forever remains
To spread
Thru memory
From memories
Throughout
The entire… domain.

Viewing

Houses and lots
And old money pots
Wrapped neatly in bundles of few.
Left in the sun
Just for fun
Grow as things justly do
Folks travel by
Buy, buy, buy
Live and then travel afar.
Viewing the world
Moon and the stars
While
Houses and lots
And old money pots
Wrapped neatly in bundles of few.
Left in the sun
Just for fun
Are growing as things justly do.

A Reason

Maybe there's a reason
The sky just seems so tall
Maybe there's a reason
And maybe not at all.
Maybe there's a reason
The ocean seems so deep
Maybe there's a reason
And maybe it's to keep.
Maybe there's a reason
The firefly lights at night
Maybe there's a reason
And maybe it's the light.
Maybe there's a reason
The wind blows far and wide
Maybe there's a reason
It's there - but yet it hides.
Maybe there's a reason
The stars shine - so beautifully
Maybe there's a reason
They watch, over you and me.
Maybe there's a reason
The sun shine by day… the moon, by night
Maybe there's a reason
Forever, celestial light.
Maybe there's a reason for everything there be
Maybe there's a reason
For you
And yes…
For me.

The Flowers - The Rainbows

The flowers are mine
They drink of the sunshine
Of the cool morning dew
Of the noon
Of the twilight
Of the shade hours too.
I also love rainbows
They mirror the storms
And enlighten the heavens
With a soft - glowing alarm
Of a coming or leaving
The minutes will tell
Oh I love the rainbows
They mirror the storms well.
Tho the flowers are mine
And the rainbows are too
For they are of love
To share
As the dew.
The twilight - the shade hours
They
Reflect...
Of love too.

A Love

The flowers knew
They were taught from the blue of distant skies
Where the sun
Was taught by years…
Of watching the universe flow by.
And the oceans had their say
In the passing of the days
As they whispered to the mountains
As they whispered to the trees
Secrets
The flowers knew.
That inside each plant
Droplet of water
Or all that is
Whatever, it may be
Is something guided spiritually -
In a very silent way
From within
Deep within.
With a love - that remains
As deep blue of the skies
On, on , and on
Forever on
As - where…
Eternity
Doth lie.

Make

To hardly imagine the unimaginable
And insist it never exists.
To hardly imagine the manageable
And insist it truly exists.
Is somewhat the same
But has missed.
The truth of it all - that is this,
The unimaginable and manageable
Are one - that together.
Make much of all
That truly - really exists.

Touches

There's magic in the beauty of a falling star
As it streaks from across the heavens
In a beauty - from afar.
There's beauty in the wind, unseen
As it moves the leaves
A special way - with a touch
That we alone can see
Quite different, at times
As waves
Of open sea.
And the love we have
Of those we see - that leave
As a falling star
In the open sky
Or the wind as it touches - leaves
Passes by.
Leaves loves
Leaves memories
As stars that fill the open sky
Beautifully - spiritual
Tho silent
Yet glow…
On and on
With a spiritual light
Forever
And ever.

In October

The morning sun in October
Revealed fog at the mountaintops
And the cool of the morning hours
Suggest Autumn's here...
Summer's not.
Tho the humming bird's here
And the cricket's around
The crow, the bee
Also seagulls abound.
The fact of life still remains
That the morning sun in October
Revealed... Autumn...
O'er the mountaintops.

Togetherness

Waters of the ocean flowing
Fast, slow, always growing
Moving as the stars.
Mountains tall they be
Mostly grains of sand
Fashioned… made - with the Creator's hand.
And of life we see
With us day to day
All in lovely ways.
Flowing as the seasons
New and then to old
Blossoms leaves, fall unfold
The cycle continues
As the Creator has planned.
And shows thru birthdays -
Happy birthday

With special love, care compassion
Togetherness, healing, all
Silently - beautifully.
While oceans flow - mountains grow
In eternal days, just… lovely.

My Garden

The roses that I see are beautiful to me
They bloom along a garden wall
Their petals flutter gently to behold.
And the color of a crimson red
Flows along the garden bed
Countless numbers of the flowers
Flourish there.
Flowers special one for me
Grew just beautiful a rose to see
Then wilted, faded, drifted quiet -
As the stars.
Now the roses blend as one
All colorful to see
And flow as ocean waves
That ripple with memories.
Silent - spiritual - beautiful…
The roses that I see
Along my garden wall
Their petals fluttering
With love…
Gently, to behold.

Where The Lilacs Bloom

Over where the lilacs bloom
There's sunshine
And a sunny natural room
Where sunbeams shimmer -
Shining perfect just right
Like stars on a soft silky summery night.
There the grass seems greener
And the other flowers too
Filled with fragrance
And fresh
Morning dew.
Tho the world is beautiful
Love reaches thru -
To everywhere.
From over where the lilacs bloom
Where there's sunshine
And a sunny natural room.
Where sunbeams shimmer
Shining perfect, just right
Like stars
Of memories.
On a soft - silky…
Summery night.

Today

A little clouds
A little sunshine
A little blue
In the sky today.
And the days passing by
In a wonderful way.
Making today

A little sunshiny
And cloudy, with blue,
Mixed in too
A really easy day -
To get use to.

Change

Isn't change lovely
Tho at times
Hard to see that way.
It changes dark to light
In a brief eternal way
And we ourselves
At that crossing.

Silently, spiritually.
Isn't change lovely
Changing change
Where - ere - we see
We see… it be.

Marriage

Marriage is lovely
Joining - joining
In its way
Both night and endless
Thru the day.
Communicating - endless
Communication
Joining - joining
Marriage… thru love.

Butterfly

I seen a butterfly in December
Perhaps - someplace this could not be
But twas seen, by more than me
And it fluttered not from
Flower to flower
But thru the air - passing…
As if to stare
And then it fluttered - ever…
In quiet on.
This butterfly seemed to me
A strange one - yet it be.
This butterfly of December
That missed the months of summer
Yet in utter quiet - fluttereth…
Strangely - on.

Mountains Tall

With start of day at sunrise
With wane of day at twilight
And night with shimmering light of the moon
There seems a time for dreams
A time for reason - a time for season
A time for mountains - we laboriously build.
A time for civilizations to rise - to crumble
A time to laugh, hate, love, or… be humble
And let in with full trust
God's love, with accomplishes wonders
Thru silence - thru beauty - thru love
Healing, faith, hope,

As doubt - fear - disappear
Dark, dawn, sunlight, twilight, moonlight
"Thru faith" appear.
While sand in grains tho small.
Builds the Creator's mountains, eternal… and…
Forever - wondrously - tall.

A Wonderful Thing

Oh

What

A

Wonderful, wonderful

Thing it would be.

Just

To

Fly as a bird

And everything see.

To go real fast

And then to rest.

In the

Ve-ry

Tallest

And

Tallest

And

Tallest

Of trees.

Oh

My

What

A

Wonderful, wonderful

Wonderful thing…

That would be.

Maybe… huh -

Just for you,

And just

For me.

In The Sunshine

Golden leaves among the green
Drifting to the ground.
Their work of beauty
Now complete
They silently drift down.
To feed the Earth
A special way
With life and leaves
And love.
Then drift away
And come again
With beauty,…
In the sunshine
From above.

Minds of Men

On the fields where flowers flow
With the wind
As it does blow.
Men engage with war machines
Against each other they do scheme.
Wages in war
That's in their minds
Only always in their minds.
When the victory it is won…
War itself is never done
It will start itself again.
Somewhere
In the minds of men.
Wars will only truly end
When they stop -
In minds of men.

Come And Go

Ask the morning
About the noon.
The noon
About twilight.
The twilight
Of evening,
The evening
Of night.
The night…
Of morning
With sunrays bright.
And find each has watched
The ages grow.
With civilizations
That…
Come and go.

The Things

Autumn sets the scene
For winter
Winter sets it up for spring
Spring prepares for coming summer
And the things that summer brings.
Like the beauty
Of the sunrise
Twilight
Evenings
Sunset too,
And the waiting for the rainbows
When we wait
They then come thru.
Of course
There's beauty
In each day
If we view it
Thru and thru
For it's filled
With love
It's way
In the things
We see
And do.

Two Men

While I was lying under a tree
In the shade
One day.
Two men walked by.
One man younger
One man older.
The old man talked
Of yesterday.
The young man listened
To what…
He had to say.

Miles Away

Under a tree
The sun
Thru the leaves
Is miles
Away.
In the blue
Of the sky.
On a real…
Clear day.

I Can See

The leaves have fallen
The world looks smaller now.
Now I can see -
I can see things.
All…
The way thru.
Can't you…
Can't you
Too.
For the leaves
Have fallen.

Dust

Dust is up high
Near the blue
Of the sky.
Dust is down low
Where people come
And go
Dust is the start…
And finish…
Of most things
We see.
While the winds
Blow dust
O'er the land
And sea.

A Flag

A flag for you
A flag for me
A flag for everyone
That's free
A flag of red and white and blue
That means that others
Thought of you.
And lived, and loved, and died for you.
A flag for you
A flag for me
A flag for everyone
That's free
Our flag of red and white and blue
A flag of love for me and you.

Tomorrow

Tomorrow never comes
It's
Always
Just one day away.
For today
Quietly
Becomes tonight.
As dark
Softly
Replaces daylight
And night remains
Till morning sun…
Lights and sky.
Heralding…
That
A new day
Is nigh.
So
Tomorrow
Is always…
Just
One day away.
From the light…
To the night…
To the light…
Of
Today.

With Light

The falling of a raindrop
On a blade
Of waving grass.
The wind upon the ocean
As wavelets
Start
And pass.
A conscious contact
In the wind
From near…
Or far
Away.
Vibrates
Of love…
Somewhat
The same
With light,
In
Its own
Way.

A Cricket

I heard a cricket chirping
In the darkness of the night.
O'er the stillness
Of the quiet,
This lone cricket's
Voice was might.
For it carried
Thru the air
Thru the stillness
That was there.
Till the echoes
And re-echoes
Sounded lovely
In the air.
One cricket...
Calling
Calling.
O'er darkness...
Stillness...
Of autumn
Air.

"Lights" Across The Fields

There's light across the fields.
I can see them over there
Shining…
Like little candles
In the dark
Against the hills.
The rows in the fields
They're long and straight
Going toward the lights.
Like the lights
Were magnets.
"Stretching the rows"
"Pulling them"
In the dark of night.
"Imagine that!"
The light in the night
Across the fields.
"Stretching the rows"
"Pulling them"
Attracting vision.
Quietly…
"Brazenly"…
Intruding the dark.
"Yet,"
There's lights across the fields.
"I can see them"

Continues.....

“Shining”
Over there.
Like little candles
Magic…
In the dark.

A Baby Cried

I heard a baby cry
It was a pleasant thing.
I heard a mother talk
Then silence it did bring.
I heard another cry
A scolding it did bring.
And then that baby cried
And cried
Till the mother came
Again.
With mother's love - a pleasant thing.

A Plan

To go back to see
What used to be
Is very hard
To do.
All has changed…
It's not the same…
And so
My friend
Have you.
For all has blended
With a plan
A universal plan…
That smoothes the days
And blends the ways.
The ages
Smile…
On you.

To Have Touched

To have touched
The wings
Of the morning.
With the hands
Of the afternoon sun.
To have touched
The mountains
And hilltops.
Then return
To retouch
Them
Again.
Is akin to youth
And age.
When they meet
As they travel
Thru life.
To have touched
The wings
Of the morning.
In the afternoon
Shades
Of life.

Cannery Row

Sometime,
When I view,
Cross the waters,
And turn the time back,
Thru my mind.
The scenes,
Round old,
Monterey Bay.
Drift back,
To the old fishing times.
When the scenes,
Round the now vacant canneries,
Were bustling,
With people around.
Awaiting,
Return of the fishing boats.
Filled,
With silver sardines,
To the brim.
Then,
The canneries,
Would bustle,
With activity,
And the machinery,
In the canneries would strain.
While the workers,

Continues.....

Processed the sardines,
Which at present,
No longer remain.
For they are gone!
Disappeared with time!
The small silver sardines.
Which once made,
Cannery Row,
A bustling,
Portal in time.
Now,
Silence fills the canneries.
But the spirit,
Drifts constantly,
With time,
And sometimes,
When folks walk.
Thru the streets,
Of,
Old Cannery Row
Old scenes,
Flash lightly,
Thru,
Their minds.

Waiting

I'm waiting for the train
I'm waiting for the train
I'm waiting for the train
To Salinas

Oh Where—oh where
Oh Where—oh where
Oh Where—oh where
In the world—is Salinas?

Its way out west
Where the broccoli grows
Its way out west
Where there's cowboys too
Its way out west
That's the place for you
Way out west in Salinas

What will you do
When you get out there
What will you do in Salinas?

Pretend I'm a cowboy
When I get out there
Ride an old grey horse
That's an old grey mare
That's what I'll do, I'll do, I'll do
That's what I'll do
When I get to Salinas

As A Mirror

As free as the wind
Doth blow
As free as the sustaining air
We know
As free as water
Softly flows
As free as parental care
That shows
The flowers, all this knows
As do the seasons
and yet all give thru -
Faith, hope, and charity
For true love is free
And needs no reason.
For love as a mirror
Reflects tho small…
Reflects the all.

Of Love

The ways of love
Are smooth as the blue
Of the skies above
Are rough like the stormy sea
Are dark as the dark
Of night
Are bright as the morning star.
But the ways of love
Has a beautiful way
To be with you - wherever you are
And are true to you
And will stay with you.
If you are with love…true too…
The you, that you -
Say you are.

These Things

Let' pretend
The stars
Are little fireflies
In the sky.
And that they light up
Just…
For some folks
Folks…
Like you and I.
Let's pretend
The moon
Is up there
Just to glow
And see.
The things that you and I
Really want
The moon to see.
Let's pretend
That day and night
And twilight comes and goes.
Only when we want it too
And only
If we know.
Then, let's pretend
That you and I
And everyone we know.

Continues.....

Knows we only
Just pretended
And…
These things
Aren't really
So.

The Little Children

Oh the little children are the ones
Where life does start to make its run.
It's what they see
And what they hear.
Their very first days
And early years.
That molds and shapes
Their very lives.
Right here before
Our watching eyes.

A Flower

A flower turns
To the rising sun
And unfolds
In a beautiful way.
As the darkness
Of night
Fades and diminishes
To the light
Of a heavenly day.
Then the flower
It seems
As a beautiful dream.
Grows lovely
In the light
Of he sun.
For the sun
Spreads love
Thru light
From above.
That turns dark
In the wondrous
Light.
And the flower unfolds
From the darkness
Of night.
To the light…
Of a heavenly
Day.

In The Spring

In the spring when the sun rises
Over the hills the flowers
Begin to grow.
The leaves comes out
And the flow with the breezes
That gently blow to and fro.
Then in summer
When all is green
Neath the warmth
Of a heavenly sun.
All that grows begins to fade
With the fading of summer sun.
Till harvest time.
With lengthening shadows
The harvest is gathered in.
And the fruit of the spring
They the grow it did bring
Gives reward as the winter
Draws nigh.
From a start in the spring
With the leaves on the trees
That grow in the summer sun
And drop in the fall
To strengthen the tree
With beauty…
Thru seasons
We feel…
We see.
From - in the spring.

A Special Highway

Brightly dusted
Golden stars
All across the sky.
In the far off
Milky Way,
Seen by you and I.
Make a special highway
In the heavens high.
Brightly dusted
Golden stars,
Seen…
By you and I.

Lasting Love

From small ripples come waves
That build the shore.
From erosion of builders
Come tiny grains of sand .
That change the Earth.
From a fallen needle
Or leaf
Come much the life.
Of a mighty tree.
_____ and _____
May your _____
Give lasting love.
Be…
Gentle as a soft breeze
Thru verdant forest.
Filled with meaning
As each tiny grain of sand.
Beautiful as the stretching
Shorelines.
And…
Grow spiritually
With
Days
Weeks
And...
Years.

Moments

Thru the quiet of the day
As the moments
Pass our way.
Thru the evening
Twilight too
And night…
As it passes thru
Submitting
To the morning bright…
May a special light
Permit you
In a special kind of way.
To savor all the present
And enjoy…
Just beautiful moments
Of every
Given
Golden day.

A Song Can Go Anywhere

A song can go anywhere
A song that our God can hear
Start the day the right way
Sing a song everyday
Sing at the break of day.

A song can go anywhere
Songs bring our God some cheer
Start your heart the right way
Sing a song in your way
A song can go anywhere.

A song can go anywhere
Sing start the day with cheer
Open up your big heart
Get a sweet brand new start
A song can go anywhere.

A song can go anywhere
Songs fill your heart with cheer
Let the spirit come in
Sing a song from within
A song can go anywhere.

A song can go anywhere
Songs make all men come near
Open your true heart wide
Sing from deep down inside
A song can go anywhere.

Continues.....

A song can go anywhere
Songs make the dark seem clear
Make the dark clouds disperse
Sing a real Christian verse
A song can go anywhere.

Chorus
Oh a song can go anywhere
Oh a song can go anywhere
A song in the morning
A song anytime
A song brings out love to share.

One Morning

I seen the moon one morning
So high in the clear blue sky.
And I seen a butterfly - fly quiet by,
Right between the moon, and I.
Maybe the moon so high, so quiet too
Watched the butterfly as it flew,
And… saw me too… maybe…
I wish, I knew. Don't you?

A Quiet Way

A rainbow
That I seen today
Spoke in a beautiful
Quiet way
And I looked
And listened
Quite…
The same.

Just A Reflection

Just a reflection
In the picture
Like a shadow on the wall.
Shining moving there to see
And then
Mysteriously - not at all.
Reflections - memories
Are akin
See them once
To feel again
Then in silence
As the wind.
They're here, they're gone
To come again.

To Everyone

For you to see the same as me
Could never, ever, ever be
For I see from deep within
Where only beauty enters in.
For you to feel the same as me
Could never, ever, ever be.
For I feel from deep within
Where only beauty enters in.
But you and I
Can true friends be
If we alone believe and see
That deep within
Our inner selves
Where love light glows
And grows and grows.
Is just the same
For everyone
Including you
And me.
When this we see
And understand
We then begin
To think
As one.
Then love can grow
As rays of sun
With radiant light
To everyone.

Your Anger

Make your anger work
In such a way
That folks can see
And they can say.
The world's a better place
To live in now.
Because that person
Showed us how.

Really Angry

When you're really, really angry
And don't know
Just what to do.
Just stomp your foot
Turn around.
Look right up
Then look down.
Take a real
Deep breath
Start back in
Then you'll do things
And you'll win.

Shalom (Within) Shalom (Without)

As the winds upon the ocean
Causes waves to drift afar
And the clouds just scatter
In the heavens high.
All this viewed with troubled mind
If peace within - one then can find
A certain quiet… within, without
Can come
Softly - spiritually
As the winds…with love.
For in these days of many choices
Tied to where the heart is free
True peace, as always -
Comes only after, achieving righteousness…
As a field of flowers grow -
Opening to the joyful rays of sunshine
There with love in warmth to grow.
And the flower with life indeed
Must be true in act and deed
To find peace - where peace as truth
Is hard to find.
Where to feel good - and to be good
Must thru love be understood
As the winds that causes
Waves and clouds
To drift afar.

Continues.....

Like peace - like love
Within - without
Are spiritually interwoven
When good or bad
Must be... individually... chosen.
And felt thru love to guard the heart
Especially as the powers within, together war -
Ever always.
For choices come with seconds, hours, years
As the people - as the flowers
As the blossoms, grasses
Softly - quietly - murmur.
In these days of... now and forever, as all... are
Tied to where the heart is free.
And with love
Must make decisions
To find peace - true peace - happiness
Within - without (shalom) (shalom).
That is free - as the seasons, as the individual reasons
That thru truth
Spiritually... releases...
To be free.

These Fields

Flowers, flowers
Fields of flowers
Picked for beauty
Some may be.
And their fragrance lingers…
Strange as Autumn
Memorably - lovely
Wondrously true.
That from these fields of flowers.
Love… shines thru.

Everyday

There's a special time everyday
And the flowers know, their way
For them to shine - and that they be
From the love of you and me.
For love you see - is what we be
And we care.
There's a special time the rainbow
Gives forth beauty as its birth
For all to see
For all it is and ever will be -
Is from the love. It beams
To you and me.
For love you see is what we be
And we care.
The knarled old tree
Is beautiful too
For the beauty it's brought
A special way
And the wisdom
It passed thru
For it survived
As the seasons - for…
Many beautiful reasons
That's silent - tho they be -
Thru you - thru me
Beautiful, as the sunshine
Thru love

Continues.....

Tho it be painful at times
Tho it be beautiful at times
Tho it be silent at times
Thru you - thru me
It flows
Beautifully
On and on
Thru each other
As we care
Forever - ever
And…
Forever.

A Kind Of Way

The cooing of the mourning dove
The breaking of the day.
Awakes the world
And passes night.
A special
Kind of way.

My Way

Vacation, vacation, vacation time
Give me a hook
And give me a live
A quiet place
Where I can be
Away from all
Society.
And it's there I'll stay
For many a day
Just passing vacation time.
My
Way.

The Rain

When lightning is flashing
Way up in the sky.
And thunder's a rumbling
Voice in the sky
When the wind is rustling
The leaves on the trees.
And the day gets dark
Like night is to me.
I like to get quiet
And go sit down.
Then soon the rain..
Will come
Pattering down.

The Swing

The swing is the place
Where I want to be
When I only
Want to be me.
I can go up in the air
And back again
Only me…
Only me…
Only me…
As high as I want
As low as I want
And nobody bothers me.
Oh…
The swing
Is the place
Where I want to be.
When I only
Want
To be
Me.

The Sun

As the sun today
Dropped low…
Behind the far off ocean's rim.
I stood and watched
Till it slowly dropped.
Becoming…
A red fiery glow
In the wide open
Spacious sky.
Then all that remained
Of that beautiful sight.
Was the twilight
That came
The ocean
The Earth
And…
Faint
Stars
In the sky.

The Sunset

Oh the sunset is so pretty
As it shines
In its own way.
And drops
Behind the ocean.
At the close
Of a beautiful day.
That it sets one's mind to thinking
And reacts
in such a way.
That those
Who view
This lovely sight.
Never...
Really forget
That special
Given
Day.

The Waves

In rushing waves
And tones
Of deep.
Waves of the ocean
Continually speak.
To shorelines…
Stretched near
And far away.
Saying…
We are one
As from birth
Stretching
Growing
With the Earth.
Filled with mystery,
Forever more.
I the waves
And you…
The shore.

The Month

Octobers just the month to see
With rainy days and skies of blue.
Crispy leaves all falling down
Crunchy, crumbly
To the ground.
With crispy air in morn and night
To start the day or night
Off right.
And farms around both big or small
Filled with harvest of the fall.
Then…
Halloween comes for everyone
"Oh" October 's just the month
To see.
Because it brings so many things
For you -
And me.

October

Sunshine hours
Flowers too
Airplanes up in the skies of blue.
Crispy leaves
September's gone
October's here
With Autumn's song
Of frosty nights
And chilly morns
Apples pumpkins
Things from farms.
Halloween
For folks to see -
Where ghosts and goblins
Creep at night
Giving all a frightful sight.
But…
October has just 31 days
Then
November comes with
Thanksgiving Day.

Little Lights

When the sun is gone
And the moon's
In the sky.
I see little lights
Start blinking
And twinkling
All, over the sky.
As the stars
Come out
Way up high.
To be with the moon
Far-rr
Up in the sky.

Black Eyed Peas

Chittlins is all right
But for me
I like collard green
And black eyed peas.
A little corn bread too
Of course will do.
And sweet potato pie
To see things thru.
Just give me this
And let me be.
But please pass me
Those black eyed peas.

Where's That Boy

Picking cotton
Driving the mules
Singing spirituals
Learning the golden rule.
Getting education
Bit by bit.
Elementary
High School
College too…
University slow
But got there too.
Where's that boy?
Hey man
"What did"
You do?

Mr. Pretty Boy

Brand new car
Brand new suit
Diamond ring
Dollar bill for loot.
Gas tank empty
Whistling dry.
Where you goin'
Mr. Pretty boy?
Can't be far
Cause…
A dollar bill's not much
In that big car.

The Fog

The fog comes ghostly quiet
Night or day
Tucks everything away
And like a dream
Drifts away
To come again
Another day.

Hey You

Hey you boy
Where you from?
Ain't you had no raisin boy?
Git back where you started from.
They ain't nothin up here to see
Cept for folks that see like me.
You boy
I'm talking to…
You…
Boy…
Git back where you started from.
I hear you talking mister
And I respect your point of view.
But there's many many things
That's planned for me
That I must do.
There's a mountain
I must climb.
A dream I must
See thru.
And when I finish
All this mister,
Maybe I'll listen
If you do.

You Are

No matter
What you say to me.
About the things
You are to be.
You really are
From what I see…
The things you
Really want to be…
And…
Nothing more.

So Much

Star light
Moon light
Oh I see
So much
Tonight.

The Years

The month of October
Brings so much fun
With crispy leaves
And such.
Because
Leaves that were new
This very Spring
Now have a crispy touch.
For months of the year
Have moved along.
And if…
The months
Themselves could tell.
Why
October would be
The ground parent month.
For its seen
The year
Move
Grad - u - ally by
In a beautiful flowing way.
And as the months
Moves along
With days
Building to years.
May they build

Continues.....

Silently
For all
And…
Beautifully
Golden treasured memories.
Filled with light, gathered -
Throughout…
The years.

The Airport

At the airport here with me
There's people everywhere to see.
Some are coming
Some are going
Some confused
It seems to me.
And the airplanes
That are here
Oh so many
Close and near.
It seems to me…
The people everywhere
I see.

Most Things

Words cover
Most things.
But for some
There is no explanation.
As when the hurt
Is deep
Beyond
All expectation.
For this
There is
No explanation.
Only silence
And
Reservation.

Stop

Sometime in the course
Of a real busy day.
Stop…
Just do nothing
Sometime in the day.
Then watch the effect
On the rest
Of the day.

A Desire

I followed paths
Across the hills
The valleys.
Across oceans
Thru the skies,
Searched
The morning winds.
For a desire within
And then…
You were there.
Tho you've left
I now…
Smile…
With the sun.

A Light

The damp of fog
Is much the same
As spray upon the ocean.
And lifts and gives a light the same,
As dark lifted, by day… in motion.

In The Fog

Ships in the fog
Drift silently,
Surrounded by
The silent sea.

To See

I wanted to see the day
But the sun was in the way
I wanted to see the night
But the moon was ever in sight
So much the same
So different too
The sun the moon
The world moves thru
Yet to see the day
To see the night
If seen with love
Is seen as right.

These Days

In these days of lovely ribbons
Tied to where the heart is free
While the seasons move along
Winter - spring
To robins song.
But the winter has a way
Of just before
It's Valentine Day
To bring a special day
To few
And this one maybe...
Just for you.
Happy Birthday

_____

And while lovely robins
Have their way
Enjoy this your special day
Of the season
Surrounded
With hearts of love.

To Remember

Summer's almost finished
But it's, still here.
With a few more days
In the month
This year.
The days are warm
Tho a little more cool
The leaves are green
And the grass is too.
The moon is full
And harvest bright
Since Labor Day's here
All but the night.
With Autumn waiting
And Jack Frost too.
Summer's almost finished
With a few days left.
To remember…
For folks
Like you -
And me too.

The Small Things

Somehow it seems it's the small -
Things in our lives
We remember as the days
go by.
The trips we took
The campfires - the 4th of July
The fishing trips - the flag
Just fooling around and wondering why.
Of course when birthdays come
And changes things
Along with a host of many other things.
Like the sunshine makes the seeds to grow
On paths of beauty
And of light.
We begin to understand
And see in a small way - the beauty
Of the many, many aspects of life
Given us thru others.
In many ways - that teach us
Leave us - lead… guide us
With touch - lack of touch - constant touch
Weakness - strength.
On paths of love, light
Absence - presence
And beautiful memories.
Small, vast, good - bad—spiritual

Continues.....

And lovely.
As we remember
As we remember
As we… with love
Remember.

A Hero

Tremendous mountains
Of cannot do
Are reduced to
Merely hills of….
Maybe one, or two.
When worry and fear
Are overcome
And courage
Gives birth to a hero
In someone.

My Friend

Be my friend
Said the wintry wind
To the grasshopper
From the summer sun.
Tho your life will be
As ice to me
And you'll sing no more
But friends we'll be,
"Be my friend"
Do you hear - be my friend.
Be my friend
Said the rambling brook
To the grasshopper
From a shady nook
Who could swim no more
Than yonder stone
Who once in the water
From the bottom shone.
Be my friend
Said the rambling brook
And we'll remain together
Forever and on
On, on and on.
No…
I must stay
Live my grasshopper way.
For your ice to me
And water too

Continues.....

Mean naught to me
When life is thru
But thank you my friends
And friends we'll be
For friends show love
True love
Is free.

Light

The loss of sunlight
Brings twilight
Then - a glimmer in darkness of light
Then –mysterious moonlight
Then—rays of dawn
Then - sunlight
To point the way
Today again

Echoes

Quiet beneath the moonlight glow
The world lay light
With a darkness glow
And the wind was quiet
With hardly a sound.
As fresh was memory
Of the recent sound
Where the Earth shook, trembled,
Shuddered then cracked
From the throes of an earthquake
That 15 seconds did last.
But destroyed as only…
Awesome wonder can behold
Like beauty a flower
To the sun does unfold.
While the world beneath tonight's moonlight glow
Lays light
With an eerie darkness glow
Ringing with echoes -
Earthquakes know.

Beautiful

The way the flowers grow
Why you should see them now
What started with the sunshine
And ended with a kiss
Has grown in understanding
And fullness such as this.
The grass around is still the same
The roots still love soft falling rain
The stem yet holds the petals too
The way it was designed to do.
But the blossoms come
And seem to show
The flowers where great beauty flows
And to remember
How to grow
With love and light
That's beautiful.
As crystal skies of blue
Very, very old
But each day very new.
And surrounded with this love
Beautiful flowers grow
Soft as moonlight
Fresh as snow.

Within

The quiet - the still
That's in a day
Befits certain hours
Of the day
With comfort still
As shady green
Of forest glen.
And other moments
Seem as rash
As desert heat
Among the thrash and gong
Of traffic blare.
But serenity is there
Flowing soft as mountain streams
Rippling… rippling
Like fleecy clouds
On moonlight nights.
Giving comfort - tho… far -
Far off the ocean waves
May crash in throe,
As distant
Ultimately
Thunder.
And personal storms rage
On - on, on and on
Into forever.
A calm resides - among it all
Deep, deep within…
Is always there - inner
And spiritually fulfilling.
As the still
That's in a day - or
The serenity of.

Continues.....

A mountain stream.
All glowing… waiting
In a light of love
Touching - comforting
Eternally
Ever and… ever
Deep within.

Because

I don't like
The way you look-
Cause you don't look
Like me.
I'll do something
You don't like,
Just you wait and see.
Because…
I don't like the way
You look.
Cause, you don't look
Like me.

Open

Thru the open window I see
Clouds at the edge of the world
And blue of sky
High over the trees
Over the mountain tops
Away - far away.
All of this so beautiful
To see
Thru my window
To the world
With love
And everyday
This silent beauty
Is always there
Waiting -
For me.

The Same

Tho the frost killed the trees
And the plants too
Strange…
They all seemed the same
When their life was thru.

Old Mr. Bullfrog

When the moon's all yellow
And pretty and full
A shinin' way up high
With stars in the sky.
Old Mr. Bullfrog
Gathers in a pond
With his friends
Just a croakin' and a bellowin'
Like the world was gonna - end
Sounds real purty tho
When the moon's all yellow
And purty and full
A shinin' way up high
With the mountains all around
Makin' shadows
Low - un-high
Under stars
Way up high
With the moon - in the sky.

Salinas

The city of Salinas, California
Rambling thru the valleys near the hills
Has a beauty that will charm you forever
Takes your love and wants you for its very own.

Oh my heart will always be in Salinas
My friends are there I'm welcome any time
Her open skies and green fields seem to call me
Call in memories to the city of my dreams.

Rodeos in the city bring the crowds out
They're classed as the very best in the land
And the warm balmy days in the valley
Makes the weather very lovely and grand.

Oh you can lose your true heart in Salinas
In the peaceful happy living of the town
Or the soft moon filled nights in the valley
Will make you want to stay in that town.

Chorus
Salinas, Salinas, Salinas
Oh you call out so clearly to me
Salinas, Salinas, Salinas
The city in the golden valley.

War

Lets go to war
Lets hit em -where it hurts
Where they'll remember
We were there
Where's the hospitals
Get em too
So they can see
We've been thorough.
Count the dead-of the human race
Buildings and civilization
Put to waste
Lets plan it good
Get all places standing
In our planning-to be destroyed,
So all will know-we've been thru.
When its all thru
When all is ready-all hands steady
Lets go to war.
Don't get their leaders
Till almost the last
Let them all see-what we can do
Get all the others
So all will know-we've got power
We're here now.
Run go hide-with great fear
At your side
And wherever you go

Continues.....

Remember-this is war.
We've planned it this way
We want it this way
It must be this way.
Don't even think of other ways
Cause this is war.
"Lets" go to war
And…
Perform this dreadful act.
But…
Only-if we must.

The Brain

So wonderful the brain
It works in spite of storms
And when the rain
Begins to fall
Or snow begins to blow
The wondrous qualities
Of the brain
Decides what, right
Or left sides
Of the brain
Must tell the body-best-
To know
So wonderful the brain

Music

I'm from the world
Of ticking clocks and watches
Those are the clock sounds
I like to hear.
From when a wind up spring
Made the hands-go round and round
To make various sounds. Of course the silence
And absence of sound
To do the same-is beautiful too
But I still like-the ticking sound
Sometime to hear
It's magic-in a way
And says, tho silently
Come-stay…
For a little while today, and hear…
The special music, perhaps-that-
Maybe only you,
Can hear

Perhaps

Can animals see-of things-
That are to be
Maybe are of things, that be.
Animals like donkeys, horses,
Cows, dogs, cats and others
That we see.
Do they at times try to
Tell us many, much
Of things that are to be.
Sometimes I wonder
I wonder, I wonder
I wonder....perhaps..
If that could be.

About The Author

I'm Al Vicent, originally from Michigan. I settled in Salinas California after military service and enjoy writing poetry to fill the vacancy of the seconds, minutes and hours that occur during the days, weeks, months and years.